I0137378

# The Hole in the Wall Ranch

## A HISTORY

TOM REA

Copyright 2010 Tom Rea

ISBN# 978-1-932636 69-7 Trade Paper

Library of Congress Control Number: 2010942096


All rights reserved.
No part of this book may be reproduced or transmitted in any form
or by any means, electronic or mechanical, including photocopying,
recording or by any information storage and retrieval system
without written permission from the publisher.

Cover Design: Antelope Design

Cover Photo: The headquarters of the Hole in the Wall Ranch,
looking south from the buffalo-jump bluff.
Photo by Dave Stoetzel

www.pronghornpress.org

*The author would like to thank the Wold family
for their generous support of the writing
and publication of this book.*

# Contents

## Chapter 3

### The British Come to Hole in the Wall 57

## Chapter 4

### Rustler Heaven 97

# Chapter 5
## Through the 20<sup>th</sup> Century    141

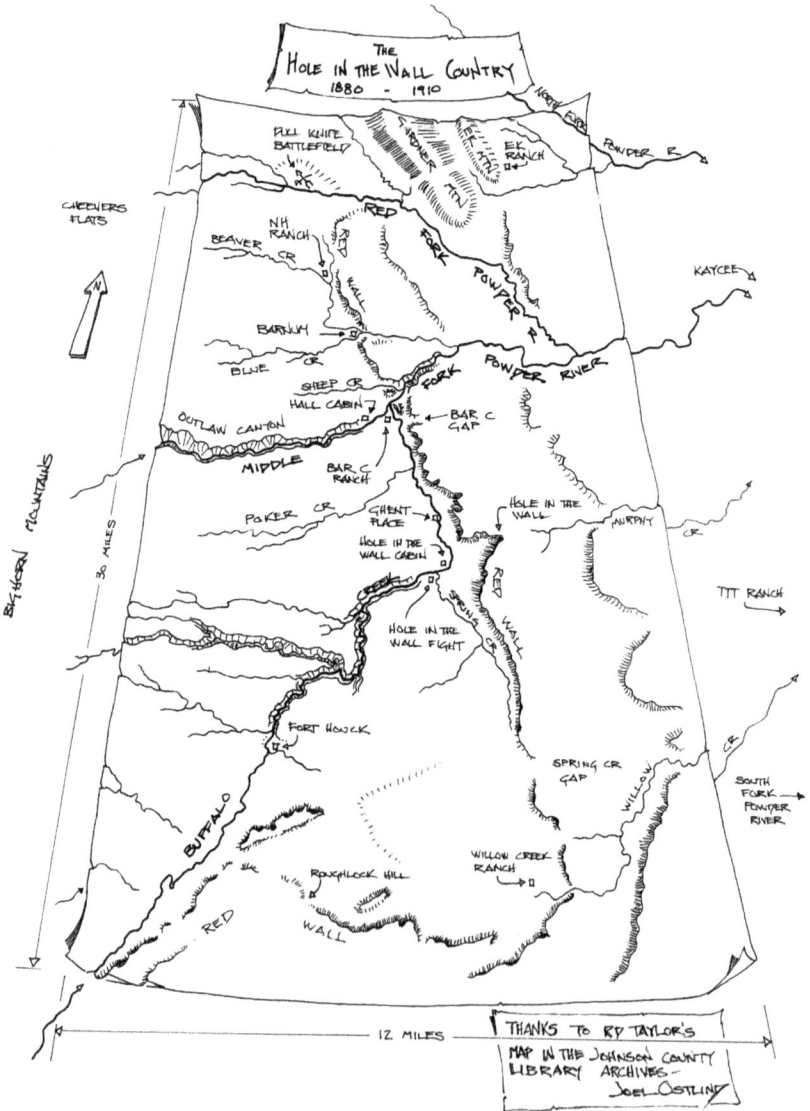

The HOLE IN THE WALL COUNTRY 1880 - 1910

## *Introduction*

# An Ancient Crossroads

The Hole in the Wall country of the Bighorn Mountains of Wyoming remains one of the West's splendid, secret places. Its cliffs are deep red, its creeks and rivers sparkle, its grass in summer grows a startling green, and its cattle thrive. People are few, skies are blue—but the red rocks dominate everything. Three hundred feet high, their sandstone cliffs and shaly slopes run north and south forty miles or more. Halfway along that distance, the Middle Fork of Powder River comes east out of a mountain canyon, meanders across the little valley, and finally cuts through the red, Red Wall.

Where the water meets the Wall, and makes its way through, lies the Hole in the Wall Ranch—a spot that, despite its grandeur, welcomes people. It has a human scale. For millennia people camped, fished, gathered food and made tools here. They left their pictures on the red rocks, ran buffalo off a nearby bluff, and butchered them at the bottom. But it wasn't just water, shade, grass and game that attracted people. It was geography. The place was a crossroads. A well-used north-south route met an equally well-used east-west route, right here.

These routes spanned half the continent. One ran along the front, that is, east side of the Rocky Mountains. It's still the route that Interstates 90 and 25 follow from Billings, Montana, to El Paso, Texas, which is only part of the same route any sensible person would take from Calgary to Chihuahua. The other route came overland from the Missouri River to the Bighorns, over them, over the Wind Rivers, around the Tetons and out to the lava plains of Idaho, and so on down the Snake and the Columbia to the Pacific.

Both saw use as game roads, trade roads, and war roads by people of all the early races of North America, red, white, brown, and black. The north-south route brought Taos whiskey up to the North Platte in fur-trade times, and twenty years later brought a freighter named John Bozeman from the Platte to the gold fields of Montana. Later, the Lakota and Cheyenne attacked, driving the Army out of the forts it had built to protect Bozeman's road. A few years later the Army returned up the same route, and drove a thousand Cheyenne from their village in a bitter, winter fight. That village was on the Red Fork of Powder River, just ten miles north of the spot where the Middle Fork meets the Red Wall.

Over the westbound route from the Missouri came the first white man to write down a careful description of the

Bighorns, a Montreal trader named Laroque, in 1805. He also described his hosts, the Crow, whom he liked, who had shown him the way, and whom he hoped to make his customers. A few years later, the same route brought the first whites to cross the continent after Lewis and Clark, a big brigade of sixty-five men, guided by a mixed-race, ex-river pirate and friend of the Crow named Edward Rose. He liked the Crow so much he moved in with them. The Bighorns remained the heart of Crow country until Cheyenne and Lakota drove out the Crow, only a few years before Bozeman came blazing his wagon road.

The same route brought the first full-bore cattlemen into the country, a pair of English brothers named Moreton and Dick Frewen. They came from the west, however, over the Bighorns, pushing, so the story goes, a herd of buffalo ahead of them through the snowdrifts. Once they saw the country they figured they could make a killing, in cattle. They imported many aristocratic guests, but made few friends locally. The only killing they made was of tens of thousands of their own animals. Overgrazing, drought, bad management, and a terrible winter combined to drive the Frewens out.

Two of their friends, meanwhile, W.C. Alston and T.W. Peters, started a ranch right where Buffalo Creek joins the Middle Fork of Powder River, where the Hole in the Wall Ranch is, now. They called it the Bar C, and the ranch kept that name through a dozen owners for a century and a quarter. Alston and Peters were driven out by the same forces that drove out the Frewens, along with another Britisher with a ranch in the Hole in the Wall country, Horace Plunkett. When these men left, they left behind a vacuum in power and economics that was filled in only slowly by men who wanted to make a living, not a killing. These men brought in

Headquarters of the Hole in the Wall Ranch today.
Steamboat Rock is the butte on the right; Castle Rock is on the left.
*Photo by Tom Rea.*

their families to do it. They intended to make communities.

But with them and their families came new ways of using the land, ways that brought them into conflict with the more feudal ways still lingering in that country. There were murders, then an organized invasion. It was called the Johnson County War, but it was more like a string of feuds. The best known of the victims, a Texan named Champion, was very nearly killed right on the Bar C, and was finally murdered a few months later at the KC Ranch, twenty miles east.

Feuds ran through the 1890s, ran north, south, east and west on these routes, and frequently crossed the old Bar C. The troubles that brought the feuds revealed a low-grade lawlessness in the country that allowed bolder thieves to thrive, for a time. These were men moving stolen horses, and sometimes stolen cash, long distances right through here, past this ranch. Butch Cassidy may have been among them; some of their deadlier, less well known friends certainly were: Harve Logan, for example, and Flat-Nosed George Currie.

At the very same time families started putting down real roots, planting gardens, making cheese, running post offices, fixing fence, running cattle and, for several decades, running more and more sheep. Descendants of these people ranch in the Hole in the Wall country today, and still have many of the same concerns—weather, climate, distant markets, the land and its capacities.

But the Hole in the Wall Ranch, the old Bar C where Buffalo Creek joins the Middle Fork, has all along remained abundant with its ancient pleasures—especially its scenery and its fish. Owner after owner since the end of feuding times acquired the ranch for pleasure as much as for profit. This was true of the merchant and banker Charles King, who bought the Bar C in 1897 (and who later became grandfather to Gerald Ford). It was true of King's successor, another banker/merchant named Alexander Cunningham. And it was true for nearly all the owners since—Burkes, Cronins, Baxters, Hartnetts, Culvers, Vests, Culvers again, Gosmans, and finally the Wolds, who have owned part of the ranch since 1980 and own all of it now.

John Wold, a geologist, longtime Wyoming oil-and-gas man and former U.S. congressman, acquired the ranch to enjoy with his family. He leaves the running of it to Jim and Kerri Richendifer, and their son Zach and Zach's family. Wold children and grandchildren, meanwhile, continue to enjoy the ranch as often as they can.

But John, 95 at this writing, loves the ranch also for its vivid past. He knows the place is important because so many interesting things happened right on the site, or at least within a day's ride, horseback. It may be the most beautiful ranch, anywhere. No brag, as the cowboys say, just fact. But thanks to the forces coming together at these ancient crossroads, the events that happened here had causes and effects that span a continent. In their particulars, they tell a history of the West.

# Chapter 1
## Beginnings

Six miles south of the Wolds' Hole in the Wall Ranch headquarters is the famous Hole in the Wall, a steep, rocky little route up through the Red Wall by way of a nearly impossible notch. Wolfers chasing wolves, and later, rustlers with their stolen stock moved routinely through this notch, according to local lore, though anyone who's seen it doubts a horse or steer could ever make it down that cliff alive.

The Hole in the Wall may have been named by early British ranchers in the area for a well-known London dive of the same name. Or it may have been named for this steep, difficult notch. Or it may have been named for the larger opening in the Red Wall made by the Middle Fork and its tributaries, or from an offhand remark of a rancher from Buffalo Creek who, asked where he was from, answered, "just a hole in the wall."[1]

In any case the Red Wall—the red sandstone of the Chugwater formation—dominates all the stories of the Hole in the Wall country. It crops out for forty miles along the southeast flank of the Bighorn Mountains, which themselves run 150 miles through northern Wyoming and bend a little way into Montana.

The creeks play a role in all the stories, too. Buffalo Creek comes east off the mountain through a limestone canyon, bends north, and runs along the base of the Red Wall for nearly half those 40 miles. The Middle Fork comes off the mountain, also through a limestone canyon. Once out of the canyon, it's joined by Buffalo Creek shortly before flowing east through the Red Wall. Continuing north, a person finds that Sheep Creek, Blue Creek, and Beaver Creek also come off the mountain through separate limestone canyons, before merging at the foot of the Wall, and joining the Middle Fork also. Finally, at the northern edge of the Hole in the Wall country, the two prongs of the Red Fork of Powder River also come west off the mountain and through limestone canyons. They join to form the Red Fork, which makes its own way east through the Wall.

All these creeks and rocks and their vivid colors are the result of ancient history of uplift and erosion, the geological forces that continue today. These forces have made it all a pretty symmetrical place. And since geology formed the land, and the land shapes all the human experience on it, it seems best to let the Earth tell its story, first.

# Geology

Hundreds of millions of years ago the land of the western United States was relatively flat, covered at times by shallow seas, at others by ash, and flooded at others by rivers overflowing their banks. These events left their different sediments, which became different strata in the rocks. Around seventy million years ago, the Bighorns and the rest of the Rocky Mountains began rising, forced up by the movement of North America's continental plate over top of the Pacific plate. Granite rocks—the much older igneous core of the mountains—pushed up from under the newer layers of sediments. As the mountain core rose, the layers above tipped back and their tops wore off, leaving the old core newly protruding, like an old turtle's back pushing up through fresh lasagna.

This rising left the oldest rocks at the top of the Bighorns, and the more recent, tipped-back ones flanking their sides in

Hikers head up into the red Chugwater Formation rocks at Hole in the Wall.
*Photo by Tom Rea.*

orderly layers. A person who drives west toward the Bighorns from Kaycee, upstream along the Middle Fork, thus drives through successively older layers—drives down through time— as he drives west through the hills along the route. Should he continue west and over the Bighorns, he would find himself driving out through the same layers but in the opposite order— driving back up through time again as he drives down the other side of the mountain.

Going down through time, the layers include the Mowry shale, from the Cretaceous period, around 100 million years old; the Morrison sandstones and mudstones from the Jurassic period, sometimes gray-green or purplish, some 140 million years old (locals sometimes call the Morrison the Gray Wall, to distinguish it from the Red Wall further west); the Sundance sandstones, also from the Jurassic, about 160 million years old, laid down under a shallow sea; and finally the hard, red Chugwater sandstones and shales of the Red Wall, rich in iron oxide, which are from the Triassic period, around 220 million years old.

One of the West's early dinosaur discoveries was in the Morrison, a few miles east of the Red Wall. In 1903, a fossil collector, W.H. Utterback, working for the Carnegie Museum in Pittsburgh, found parts of a skull, the front limbs, and a large portion of the tail of two specimens of the long-tailed, long-necked herbivore *Diplodocus* in Morrison rocks near where the Red Fork joins the Middle Fork about five miles east of the Red Wall. Utterback found more bones at another quarry on the old EK Ranch, several miles further north.[2]

The Sundance Formation, one layer older than the Morrison, is rich in fossils, too, almost all of them marine fossils. These include the plentiful, bullet-shaped belemnites, an inch or two long, the remains of a kind of squid.

Dinosaurs died out not long after the Rocky Mountains began to rise. Mammals grew in size and diversity to fill the empty ecological niches. About two million years ago, during the Pleistocene era, the north polar ice cap began a series of advances and retreats. North American mammals that may have roamed the Hole in the Wall Ranch included horses, camels, cheetahs, pronghorns, mammoths, mastodons, beavers the size of bears, and *Bison antiquus*, a quarter again as large as the modern *Bison bison*. And before long, people lived along the Middle Fork, too.

# Archeology

Scholars continue to argue about when humans first came to the Americas, but generally they agree that by thirteen thousand years ago, early people making similar stone projectile points had dispersed across the continent. These points, named Clovis points for the site in New Mexico where they were first discovered, are generally four or five inches long, flaked on both sides, with a concave groove on both sides of the point for the shaft of a thrusting stick or spear. The grooves run from the base about a third the length of the point. Clovis points have turned up in the Bighorns, though none so far have turned up along the Middle Fork or its tributaries.

Later ancient people made smaller points with wider, shallower grooves for the spear shaft. These Folsom points show up in the archaeological record of North America between 11,500 and 10,000 years ago. Wyoming archeologist Julie

Glenn Sweem in the rock shelter he excavated in 1959 and 1960,
near Outlaw Canyon, 1972.
*Courtesy of Glenn Sweem Collection/Scott Burgan*

Francis, who led crews surveying the Middle Fork sites in the 1980s, believes it's likely that people lived along the stream at least since Folsom times.[3]

A systematic understanding of these ancient Middle Fork residents began in 1950. Spurred by a proposal to dam the stream four miles east of where it cuts through the Red Wall, the federal government commissioned a series of archaeological surveys. Storing water for irrigators twenty miles downstream, the dam would have flooded eighteen hundred acres along the Middle Fork and Beaver Creek, which makes a separate cut through the Red Wall about three miles north of the Hole in the Wall ranch headquarters. The center of the reservoir would have been about at the Beaver Creek-Middle Fork confluence, with flooded arms backing up both creeks.

The archaeology work was commissioned by the Missouri River Basin Survey, an effort of the Smithsonian Institution, the National Park Service, and the Army Corps of Engineers. Two archeologists identified seventeen sites of interest on the Middle Fork. One included dinosaur bones, in the Morrison formation; the other sites were archaeological, and included a rock shelter, three rock-art sites, one stone circle—a tipi ring—and eleven prehistoric campsites. Each of these sites was given a number and described. The report was published in 1953.[4] The Corps of Engineers, however, had other priorities and no dam was built.

In 1959 and 1960, Glenn Sweem, a railroad man and amateur archeologist from Sheridan, Wyoming led teams that excavated the floor of a cave—a rock shelter, archaeologists call it—a few miles up the mountain west of the ranch headquarters. Sweem and his friend Don Grey, a science instructor at Sheridan College, were founders of the Wyoming Archaeological Society. They got permission to excavate the site from Ethel Taylor and her son Garvin Taylor, owners of the Blue Creek ranch, as the cave, on public land, was part of a Blue Creek Ranch grazing lease. That lease is now part of the Wolds' Hole in the Wall Ranch.

The cave is filled with pictographs and petroglyphs. It lies in the Tensleep sandstone, not far from the south rim of the Middle Fork's limestone canyon, known generally as Outlaw Canyon. The cave looks west and south over a gently rising field of grass and sagebrush at about sixty-five hundred feet. At forty feet wide, seven feet high at the highest, and perhaps fifteen feet deep, the cave was the biggest and most accessible of many shelters Sweem and Grey knew about after several summers exploring the Hole in the Wall country.

In the summer of 1959, Sweem and his volunteers excavated the cave floor, and sketched and photographed the rock art. They found six distinct soil layers, all but the lowest of which contained signs of human occupation. Hundreds of artifacts turned up, mostly stone scrapers, blades, awls, two manos, or grinding stones, and several styles of projectile points. There were also hearths and firepits in the top five layers. Layer two revealed a low mound of stones along the southern half of the shelter's opening, apparently a foundation for a windbreak of brush, which later had burned.

Sweem and Grey figured the site must have been occupied often, from around seventy-five hundred years ago right up to a century or two before European contact. A radiocarbon date from a fire pit low in the fourth layer came in at 4,963 years before the present, plus or minus 240 years.[5] Theirs was the most detailed work ever done on a single archaeology site on the Hole- in-the-Wall Ranch.

But it took a second, broader survey to show the valley's rich potential for records of the human past. In the mid-1970s, the proposal to dam the Middle Fork resurfaced, with a new market for the water that the dam would have stored. Exxon needed water for a proposed synthetic-fuel-from-coal operation based on Powder River coals. The survey work this time fell to the Office of the Wyoming State Archaeologist, and was supervised by Julie Francis, a professional archaeologist.

Francis and her team relocated the sites from the 1953 report, and others that had been found since that time. The team eventually reported eighty-four known prehistoric sites along the Middle Fork and Beaver Creek that would be flooded if the dam were built. About a third of those are on what's now the Hole in the Wall Ranch. Francis' crews ran test excavations at eleven sites. "Really," she says now, "we just scratched the surface." But the potential was enormous.[6] The archaeologists were looking at an unopened book that could be ten thousand years long.

Most archaeology in the West, like Sweem's and Grey's at the rock shelter, has been done at single spots, which may have been used thousands of years for one purpose, but which are quite isolated from each other. But the many sites along Beaver Creek and the Middle Fork offered much more. They could show how people made their livings differently at different sites and seasons, how they may have worked together to hunt, gather, cook and make tools, and how they changed survival tactics over time in response to changing conditions.

All the sites showed signs of human occupation. Radiocarbon dates from twenty-eight samples from the eleven sites excavated by Francis and her crews ran back five thousand years or more. Francis is confident, however, that people have lived along the Middle Fork at least ten thousand years. And some had an active buffalo-killing operation.

Spring Creek winds roughly parallel to the Middle Fork

for a mile or so, then joins the larger creek just after its
confluence with Buffalo Creek. Not long after they bought the
ranch, the Wolds built a comfortable house on a terrace that
rises ten or fifteen feet above the level of Spring Creek, and they
also widened the creek in spots to encourage trout pools. Just
north of the house lies a long, narrow, flat-topped, east-west-
running bluff. The bluff is a layer of Chugwater sandstone
overlain by a hard, Pleistocene conglomerate.

In the spring of 1985, John Wold asked Casper geologist
and archaeologist John Albanese to analyze some tipi rings on
the bluff. Albanese noticed two converging lines of low rock
cairns, running from northwest to southeast, and coming nearly
to a point near the south edge of the bluff,  near the east end.
It takes a trained eye to see the cairns in the grass; they're low
heaps of rocks, perhaps two feet in diameter and six or eight
inches high. They converge above a drop of about ninety feet
to the creekside terrace below the bluff.

Albanese had a pretty good idea of what he was seeing;
with shovels he and Wold dug four small holes on the slope
below where the lines of cairns converged. Thirty centimeters
down, in all four holes, they found bison bones. These, Albanese
could tell, had been butchered. They'd found a buffalo jump.
Francis' crew that spring just happened to be working a few
hundred yards downstream. Excited by Albanese's find, these
people volunteered their evenings for some preliminary work
on the jump.

Quickly they confirmed the presence of three of the
classic components of a bison-kill site: the drive lines of cairns;
the area where the animals, after their fall, were killed if
still alive; and a processing area slightly downstream where
they were skinned and cut up. Most likely the animals were
herded up onto the top of the bluff from the northwest side,

and then south across the bluff into the narrowing Vee between the V-shaped drive lines. Drivers would have emerged from behind the north slope to frighten the animals down the vee. Each wing of the vee has about twenty cairns, ten or fifteen meters apart, with the distance between them shortening as the animals approached the cliff edge. Shortly before the edge is a short, steep slope, which may have confused and further panicked the bison before they went over the cliff. The thirty-meter fall would have killed most, and the rest would have been easy to finish off.

The volunteers excavated a hole one meter square next to the lowest of the four test holes. About forty centimeters down, they found bison vertebrae, ribs, and two lower jawbones, all with signs of human butchering and cooking—charcoal on the bones, flakes of chert from tool sharpening, etc. In earlier years, ranch hands had gathered a number of bones from under a big boulder just south of the crew's excavation hole. A skull had a hole knocked into its brain case, a common sign, Albanese knew, that the animal had been butchered by humans.

A cutbank along Spring Creek slightly downstream showed more butchered bison bone, bone flakes, and chert flakes. Charcoal levels showing in the bank suggested different layers of use over time. The crews therefore dug another one-meter-square test hole just north of the cutbank, hoping for more big bones, and artifacts. Twenty-five centimeters down they did find some charcoal staining on the bone splinters, and more chert flakes.

From this preliminary work, Albanese came to feel he was looking at a kill operation that was never very large. The hunt could easily have been run by just one or two families, in contrast to hunts at big sites like the Vore buffalo jump east of Sundance, Wyoming. Small sites may in fact have been much more common. But few are known, and the Hole in the Wall site is unusual in having a processing site nearby. A radiocarbon date on the bones placed the site in the Late Prehistoric period, about five hundred years ago.[7]

# The Art of the Ancients

Near where the Middle Fork makes its way through the Red Wall, on a piece of the ranch acquired by the Wolds from the Gosman and Culver families in 2006, three panels of rock art offer clues to the interior lives of the early people. The sites are well protected; even in December, winter sun falls full on the warm, red, south-facing sandstone of the rock faces. The images are clearly personal, and imaginative. Cliff swallows' gourd-shaped mud nests, empty in winter, cluster in the little overhangs above the rock art.

The first site is a small panel of several stenciled hands, and what may be a stencil of an atlatl, a carved stick that notches into the back end of a dart or spear, to lever extra power for the thrower. The images appear to have been made with white clay, probably blown out of the mouth of the artist and splattering around an outstretched hand, leaving the negative image of the hand on the red, smooth rock. Each hand is different from the rest. The panel is under an overhang fifteen feet or so above a steep slope—a hard spot to get to.

The second panel stretches 150 yards along several connected rock faces a few hundred yards downstream. Some of the images are incised—cut into the rock. Others are painted on. They include lizards, bear claws, the head of a bighorn sheep, a possible shaman in a horned headdress, and other human figures, with V-necks, shields, and often with fingers on their hands.

Stenciled hands, rare in rock art of the northern plains, dominate at least two sites along the Middle Fork of Powder River. *Tom Rea photo.*

Furthest downstream and across a draw is a final panel, with nineteen stenciled hands at varying heights above the ground and again, each hand different from the others. These outlines include wrists and forearms, too.

Handprints are common in rock art worldwide. In North America they show up everywhere but the Pacific Northwest. Stenciled hands are less common; images with wrists and forearms showing are even rarer. Image groups like these are most common on the Southern Plains where, Francis writes, "they are believed to represent individuals." Clearly that's the case here. Nineteen different hand shapes imply at least nineteen different people. Placing a hand inside the outline, a person almost feels he can touch them.[8]

Though their numbers were never large, perhaps never more than the few hundred who even now ranch along the Middle Fork and its tributaries, Francis believes the ancient peoples' populations grew slowly and steadily over that time. Probably the populations shrank during the great drought from around five thousand to three thousand years ago, and during climate fluctuations in the Late Prehistoric period from about fifteen hundred to five hundred years ago. Other High Plains archaeology has demonstrated that these events changed where and how people lived. But in general, Francis says, it's likely there was a small Indian population on the Middle Fork and its tributaries that peaked not long before first contact with white people, around two hundred years ago.[9]

*Chapter 2*

Crow and Cheyenne Country

By 1600, Europeans were in constant, steady contact with North America. By the middle of the following century, European trade had penetrated deep into the interior. In 1742 and 1743, the Canadian French traders Louis and François de la Vérendrye explored west and south from the Mandan villages at the big bend of the upper Missouri River, in what's now central North Dakota. They came in sight of mountains that, if not the Black Hills, were the Bighorn Mountains of Wyoming. En route they encountered a tribe of horse Indians they named *les Beaux Hommes*, the handsome men, who probably were Crow.

The Bighorns at that time were the heart of Crow Country. A hill at the base of *Awaxaawakússawishe*, Cloud Peak, highest mountain in the range, was where the Crow say the twinkling stars came down and became the sacred tobacco seeds. Near them the Crow more or less settled down after decades of wandering.[1] From white reports, we know the Crow first brought Euro-Americans into the Hole in the Wall country.

In 1805, the fur trader François-Antoine Larocque spent

the summer with the Crow, traveling west like the Vérendryes from the Mandan villages but keeping a much more detailed journal. Larocque was working for the Northwest Company, a combination of French-and English-speaking merchants out of Montreal.

His journal, which he kept in English, is the first written description of the Crow and their country by a Euro-American. He noted their superb horsemanship, their cleanliness, their relatively light skin, the men's elaborate care for their appearance, the people's unusual willingness, compared to other tribes, to care for their old and disabled—probably, he thought, because transport was easy on their many horses. He remarked on their sociability, on husbands' sometimes violent jealousy of wives, on the fact that women did most of the work. He described a strictly managed buffalo hunt and a scalp dance after a skirmish with Assiniboines.

Larocque and the Crow traveled on a well-used route west from the Mandan villages, across the Little Missouri to Powder River in what's now southeastern Montana, southwest up Powder River and up (probably) Clear Creek to the foot of the Bighorns near present Buffalo, Wyoming.[2]

Larocque counted around twenty-four hundred people in the tribe that summer. He added that this number must have represented a remnant of a much larger Crow Nation. Their numbers were so much reduced by smallpox from earlier times, he noted, that all now traveled together most of the year for safety.[3] In more populous times they would have spent more of the year split into smaller bands. They treated the Bighorns, the Yellowstone River valley and the valleys of its tributaries as their own country; any non-Crow in those places they regarded as potential enemies—except for whites.

# Edward Rose,
# the Crow, and the Astorians

The first glimmer of a description of the Hole in the Wall country appears in frontier literature in an account from 1811, when the Crow guided a brigade of American traders and fur trappers over the Bighorns. These were the Astorians, the first Americans to cross the continent after Lewis and Clark. They were in the employ of John Jacob Astor of New York, king of the American fur trade. Their brigade leader, Wilson Price Hunt, kept a diary, which allows us to follow their route, and their difficulties, in fairly close detail.

When Lewis and Clark returned from the Pacific in 1806, Astor immediately began thinking of a way to expand across the continent—and around the world. In 1810 he sent a ship loaded with trade goods to Oregon by way of Cape Horn.

He sent a second party with trade goods overland. These overland Astorians were told to meet the seaborne traders at the mouth of the Columbia River, and scout good trading sites along the way.

On the mouth of the Columbia, they planned to establish a post where Astor's ships could pick up American furs, take them across the Pacific, trade them for Chinese silks and porcelain, head around Africa, trade in Europe where demand for Chinese goods was high, and return to New York. Profits could be enormous.[4]

Wilson Price Hunt, a St. Louis merchant and Astor partner, recruited hunters, horse packers, and voyageurs. Together with a few other Astor partners, the party numbered sixty-five. Warned of hostile Blackfeet in what's now Montana, they took a more southern route than Lewis and Clark, starting west from the Arikara villages on the Missouri River in what's now Nebraska. At the villages they bought horses and hired one of the most flamboyant figures in the entire Rocky Mountain fur trade, a former river pirate named Edward Rose. Rose was a longtime friend of the Crow.

Reportedly one-quarter Cherokee, one-quarter African, and one-half white, Rose grew up in the river trade near Louisville, on the Ohio, fighting, brawling, and losing the tip of his nose to the teeth of a big Chillicothean. In 1807, he went up the Missouri and the Yellowstone with the trader Manuel Lisa. Lisa sent him into the Bighorns to make customers of the Crow.

But instead of trading for furs that winter, Rose simply gave the Crow all the trade goods Lisa had consigned to him, asking nothing material in return. He may have intuited the commercial potential of Indian generosity, an intuition that his white colleagues lacked.

The next spring, Rose returned empty handed to Lisa's post at the mouth of the Bighorn River—with neither trade goods, nor beaver pelts to show for them. There was a confrontation; Lisa was furious and the two came to blows. Bystanders had to pull them apart. Shaken, Lisa retreated quickly to the keelboat, already manned, loaded with furs, and about to shove off for St. Louis. Rose grabbed an onshore swivel gun, touched it off with his pipe, and raked the boat deck with grapeshot. Fortunately, every ball hit the cargo box. No one was hurt. Fifteen men had to pull Rose off the gun before he could fire a second round.

The keelboat shoved off; Rose talked or bullied the men still at the post out of a new load of trade goods, and headed back into the mountains. He spent much of the next two years among the Crow, cementing their friendship with his generosity and charisma, and building a reputation, too, as a war leader. His hosts changed his Crow name from Cut Nose to Five Scalps. Over the years he interpreted and traded with various trapping brigades, and continued wintering with the Crow. People thought of him as smart, violent, generous, and unpredictable—a useful reputation.[5] After traveling with him for a few weeks in the summer of 1811, Wilson Price Hunt described Rose as "a very bad fellow full of daring."[6] In the Hole in the Wall country, Hunt's opinion would change.

Most historians agree that Hunt, Rose, and the Astorians traveled, like Larocque, up Powder River and Clear Creek about to where Buffalo is now. They halted there for two days to hunt buffalo and dry the meat.

The next day two Crow Indians appeared. The following

day, a larger party including children showed up, and invited
the Astorians to follow them to their camp. They were now
on the east flank of the Bighorns, between present-day Buffalo
and Kaycee. Hunt was impressed by Crow horsemanship:
"Even the children do not go afoot. These Indians are such
good horsemen that they climb and descend the mountains
and rocks as though they were galloping in a riding school."
The Astorians bought robes and pelts with their trade goods, and
swapped their tired horses for fresh ones.

But the Astorians had been warned that once Rose got
close to the Crow, he'd be likely to take off with all the goods he
could carry—and men too, and horses; Hunt worried about a
full-scale desertion of his trappers and voyageurs. He didn't
panic, however; he just paid close attention. "We resolved to
forestall him," he wrote.

Without the Crow, the Astorians continued south another
day along the front of the mountain, halting more than likely
on Crazy Woman Creek, or on the North Fork of Powder River.
On September 3, 1811, they made a half-hearted, half-day
attempt to find a way over the mountain. Hunt confessed in
his journal his worries about Rose's trustworthiness. Rather
than risk a mutiny, he decided to try to buy Rose off.

He suggested Rose just stay in the mountains with the
Crow, and offered him a severance package: half a year's
pay in trade goods, a horse, and three beaver traps. He was
offering Rose tools to make a living indefinitely, as a trapper.
Rose agreed, and the potential mutiny dissolved. But still
the Astorians didn't know the way over the mountains.

On September 4, the Crow headman sent Rose right
back to the Astorians "to place us on the right road,
which crossed the mountains and which was shorter and
better," Hunt wrote. It was a generous gesture by the

headman and perhaps by Rose, too. Just as sociable as Larocque had described them a few years earlier, more Crow soon joined the party, and all continued over the mountain. They camped near the headwaters of a stream on the Bighorns' eastern slope.[7]

Hunt's journal is not specific enough to show his route precisely, but many historians have speculated about it. One of the best-known historians seems almost certainly wrong; he has Hunt crossing the mountains too far north, and climbing two thousand feet in elevation higher than necessary.[8] A more likely route would have been up the Middle Fork of the Powder, and then up Beaver Creek or Blue Creek, or up the Middle Fork itself. A clergyman history buff from Oregon who retraced their route in 1911 suggested it was Beaver Creek.[9] Rock cairns along Blue Creek and the Middle Fork, modern archaeologists say, almost certainly show that they were well-used Indian routes for a long time. Most likely the Astorians were following one of these.[10]

We do know that from earliest times, a route ran north to south along the east flank of the Bighorns; much of this later became the Bozeman Trail. After crossing Crazy Woman Creek and the North Fork of the Powder, however, it hugged the mountain more closely, crossing the Red Fork and then running south behind the Red Wall all the way to where Arminto is now. This was a main north-south Indian route, called the Sioux Trail, or the Old Sioux Trail by local ranchers well into the 20th century.[11]

The existence of these trails also implies strongly that the area around Barnum and the present Hole in the Wall Ranch has been a crossroads for thousands of years, and goes a long way toward explaining why there are so many archeological sites where the Middle Fork, Buffalo Creek, and

Beaver Creek all come together.

It's safe to assume, then, that Crows guided the Astorians along what's now called the Sioux Trail, and then up and over the mountain via Beaver Creek, Blue Creek, or the Middle Fork. Any of these routes would have taken them through the Red Wall at present Barnum, and the Middle Fork route, of course, would have taken them right through the Hole in the Wall Ranch.

On the seventh of September 1811, the Crow-led Astorians most likely traveled down Little Canyon Creek on the west side of the Bighorns to where it joins the Nowood River at a modern crossroads called Big Trails.[12] From here they turned south up the Nowood, probably crossing the low Cottonwood Pass to the drainage of Badwater Creek, and then west down Badwater to the Bighorn River, up the Bighorn and Wind rivers, and over the Continental Divide by way of Union Pass.

During this last leg after a final horse trade, the Crows left the Astorians and headed south to the North Platte to visit some Arapaho Indians there.[13] Rose exits Hunt's narrative at this point, though other fur-trade journals show him a source of energy and leadership among the Crow for another twenty years.[14]

Hunt and most of his Astorians straggled into the new post of Astoria at the mouth of the Columbia in the winter and spring of 1812. Their support ship the *Tonquin* had arrived nearly a year before, but on a trading voyage north along the coast, its crew and insolent captain were killed by Indians near Vancouver Island. The partners decided to send a small party east with dispatches for Astor in New York. These men crossed the continent successfully by way of South Pass around the southern end of the Wind River Mountains, an easier, shorter route previously unknown to whites. Later the route was to be called the Oregon Trail.

War broke out with Britain in 1812, and Astor lost Astoria. Depression followed, and the Missouri River fur trade stalled. The South Pass route went dormant until the early 1820s, when the beaver trade picked up again, in earnest.

# Beaver on Powder River

By the 1830s, the trappers, traders, and Indians were taking a hundred thousand beaver a year out of the mountains, and the rendezvous system—an annual trade fair held most years on the Green River west of the Continental Divide—was well established.[15] With the center of trappers' commerce on the Green, the Bighorns and the Hole in the Wall country were definitely a fur-trade sideshow. Still, some hot competition found its way to Powder River.

In 1833, a Portuguese trader and trapper, Antonio Montero, switched his allegiance away from the American Fur Company, the biggest operator in the Rockies, to a latecomer to the business named Benjamin Bonneville, a French-born U.S. Army captain. In 1834, Bonneville sent Montero and fifty men into Crow country on Powder River. They fell in with the Crow, who treated them well and persuaded them to stay the winter.

Things had gotten harder for the Crow. Intertribal war, which in Larocque's time had been something like sport, was by now chronic and dangerous. The Crow's enemies, the Lakota, Cheyenne, and Blackfeet were more populous and better armed. Smallpox was back, too; early in the 1830s an epidemic took as many as half the Crow, and left the rest in disarray.[16]

In late summer 1834, after an unsuccessful attempt to make war on some Missouri River traders supplying the Blackfeet, the Crow must have been delighted to find Montero and his brigade of trappers and traders on Powder River. The trappers built their post about six miles east of present Kaycee. There was a palisade of cottonwood logs 100 feet by 150 feet, with trading houses inside and a corral attached. Never before had trade goods been available so deep in Crow territory. Bonneville kept the little post supplied.[17]

But he had come into the beaver trade too late. Beaver numbers by this time were dwindling and everyone knew it; "trapped out" was the term the trappers used. The fall in supply was accompanied by a fall in demand: silk hats for men replaced beaver as the style across Europe and in the eastern U.S.

Bonneville supported a brigade for another year at what came to be called the Portuguese Houses. The following year he closed out his business with several of his lieutenants, probably including Montero. Montero then seems to have tried to raise a trading outfit on his own credit. It wasn't enough. In December, Jim Bridger and three hundred men showed up on Powder River. It was an enormous brigade, if that figure is true, and represents a kind of industrialization of the beaver hunt. Bridger's intention can only have been to drive Montero out of business, probably by capturing his

Crow customers and killing all the remaining beaver on Powder River and its tributaries. By the spring of 1837, business at the Portuguese Houses was nearly dead.[18]

The last Green River rendezvous was in 1840. It had been an efficient system for a while, not just at bringing pelts out of the mountains, but at changing people's lives. With the beaver gone, many Rocky Mountain meadows, once made moist and lush by beaver dams, became dry and hard. With the beaver trade gone, people of all races gradually turned to a growing trade in buffalo hides. And more and more white people kept coming into the West by Missouri River steamboat—head of navigation was Fort Benton in central Montana—or crossing the West on the Oregon-California-Mormon Trail.

# Disease, Treaties, and War

These pressures exacted a heavy toll on the native people. When white men's diseases weakened them, enemy tribes attacked. Whites tried to impose peace through treaties, then broke the treaties and, after more war, called for more treaties.

When smallpox swept up the rivers in 1838, at the speed of steamboats now, it wiped out the Mandans as a people and decimated the other river tribes. The Mandans' populous mud-house villages at the upper bend of the Missouri had been continental trading centers for well over a century. The Vérendryes, Larocque, and Lewis and Clark had all stopped there to refit. In 1838, the Crow got advance word of the approach of the plague, and managed to avoid it.[19] They were less successful in the fall of 1851, when some Crow on Powder River caught smallpox from some Shoshone who'd picked it up from California-bound whites on the Oregon-

California Trail along the North Platte.[20]

Earlier that year, the Crow were present at the negotiations near Fort Laramie for the Treaty of 1851, the first to outline separate territories for the tribes of the northern plains and Rockies. The Crow signed the treaty, but Indians' understanding of ownership was so different from whites' that none of the tribes saw the full implication: once you draw a boundary around a piece of land, you make the land an object, a commodity. From then on, it can be lost, stolen, or sold.

A Crow orator, Sits-in-the-Middle-of-the-Land, asked his listeners to imagine a tipi, with one of its four base poles in the Wind River Mountains, one in the Black Hills of Dakota, one planted at the Yellowstone-Missouri confluence, and one at the Three Forks of the Missouri. These are the corners of the Crow lodge, he said. His geography puts Cloud Peak, highest peak of the Bighorns, right about at the middle of a concept of Crow territory that survives among the Crow today.[21] That is, the Hole in the Wall country is still part of Crow country, as far as the Crow are concerned.

When the American Fur Company clerk Edward Denig wrote at length of the Crow in 1856, he portrayed them as poorer, sicker, and more grief-stricken than Larocque had, fifty years earlier. He reported 460 lodges of Crow—around thirty-seven hundred people. This would mean they had recovered since Larocque's time but still were nowhere near the pre-smallpox levels of the 1700s.

By the 1850s, southern bands of Crow still summered in the Hole in the Wall country on the headwaters of Powder River, or along Wind River. Oglala Lakota (Sioux), meanwhile, were moving west across the Powder. Along that border and elsewhere, Oglala and Crow had been at war as long as anyone could remember. The Crow, outnumbered and outgunned, retreated north. Government negotiators at a second Fort Laramie treaty, in 1868, drew a new, much smaller Crow country, placing the Crow on a reservation north of the new Montana line and south of the Yellowstone. There their descendants remain, on a fraction of the space described by Sits-in-the-Middle-of-the-Land.

So it was that when white miners and traders pushed a road from the Oregon Trail north through the Powder River country, it was Cheyenne and Oglala, defending land they had controlled for only a few years, who resisted. The new road followed older trails from the North Platte to the Yellowstone. When John Bozeman first tried it in 1863, bound for the new gold fields of western Montana, the Oglala warned him not to continue past Powder River. So instead of continuing north he turned west up the Powder, then back south again to the Emigrant Road. That trip took him through the Red Wall and probably up Buffalo Creek—right through what later would become the Hole in the Wall Ranch.[22]

Montana-bound miners kept using Bozeman's route, however, and Cheyenne and Lakota resistance to the travelers hardened into war. In 1866, the Army built forts Phil Kearny near present Story, Wyoming, and C.F. Smith in Montana to protect the miners. Indian raids, led by Red Cloud, an Oglala, became constant. One Indian victory, when Capt. William Fetterman and all eighty men under him were rubbed out by Oglala and Cheyenne near Fort Phil Kearny in December of that year, sent shock waves through the Army and along the frontier. In 1868, with the nearly finished Union Pacific Railroad about to open a shorter, safer route to the Montana mines, the Army sued for peace and abandoned the forts. The Cheyenne and

Lakota burned them as soon as the troops left. The same treaty that gave the Crow the land north of the Montana line established a Great Sioux (Lakota) Reservation in the western half of what's now North and South Dakota. The same treaty also designated the country east of the Bighorns and west of the Dakota line as unceded Indian territory. It was some of the last good buffalo ground in the West. The Lakota and Cheyenne figured they'd be allowed to hunt there indefinitely.

But the peace didn't last. Gold was discovered in the Black Hills in 1874, and before long, the government was pressuring the Lakota to sell the Hills and move permanently onto the reservations. Some, including Red Cloud, figured it was better to sell than to have the land simply taken from them. Others, including Crazy Horse, could not see that they'd done anything contrary to their treaty promises, and planned to stay in the buffalo country.

Late in the fall of 1875, the government issued an ultimatum: any Lakota or Cheyenne who hadn't come in to the reservations by the end of January 1876, would be considered hostile. There was no way, in winter, for this message even to reach most of the villages still out away from the reservation.

That spring, the Army mounted the most famous campaign of the Indian wars, with troops under Gen. Alfred Terry traveling up the Yellowstone by steamboat, troops under Gen. George Crook traveling north over the Bozeman Trail from Fort Fetterman on the North Platte, and the Seventh Cavalry under Lt. Col. George A. Custer traveling overland—traveling roughly the same route Larocque took in 1805—from Fort Abraham Lincoln on the Missouri River in Dakota Territory, where the Mandan villages used to be.

The three prongs of this pincer movement never met, however. Lakota and Cheyenne warriors stopped Crook and his Shoshone allies on Rosebud Creek, in southern Montana. Custer and half of his command were killed a week later by the same Indians on the Little Bighorn. Terry arrived only after the tribes had dispersed.

In November, Crook again set out north from Fort Fetterman, this time with sixteen hundred infantry and cavalry, and about four hundred Indian allies, including one hundred Pawnee, about one hundred Shoshone, and smaller numbers of Arapaho, Lakota, and Cheyenne. The weather was bitter cold.

Crook's army had crossed Powder River and was camped on Crazy Woman Creek, northwest of present-day Kaycee, when the scouts brought word of a village of Cheyenne camped at the head of the Red Fork of Powder River (the present Graves ranch, ten miles north of the Hole in the Wall Ranch.) The soldiers had been hoping to catch up with Crazy Horse's village much farther north, but here was closer prey.

Crook sent his cavalry under Colonel Ranald MacKenzie along with all the Indian allies to attack the Cheyenne village. They marched all night through deep canyons and slippery snow.

Dull Knife's people had known there were soldiers in the area; in fact they had left a camp on the Middle Fork just days before for the more remote ground on the Red Fork. Many in the camp were packed and ready to flee, but a strong faction—the Kit Foxes warrior society—insisted the people stay and dance a victory dance to celebrate a recent, successful raid on a Shoshone village. The dancing went on all night, with the warriors and their families heading for bed only as dawn was breaking.

After the drums stopped, the soldiers and their Indian

The Graves Ranch and Dull Knife battlefield, on the Red Fork of Powder River, from the air. The soldiers advanced from the right, the Cheyenne were camped along the creek in the middle ground, and escaped up the deep ravine on the upper left. *Tom Rea photo; Peter Wold, pilot.*

allies attacked. The Cheyenne fought a smart, stubborn rearguard action all day, protecting their families as the women, children, and old people escaped up a canyon into the mountains. Nearly all the Cheyenne managed to escape with their lives; only around twenty-five warriors were killed out of a village of nine hundred or a thousand people. The Pawnee and the soldiers burned all the tipis, however, along with the Cheyenne's clothing, buffalo robes, and their household goods, and captured nearly all their horses.

North along the east flank of the Bighorns and then out onto the plains, the Cheyenne made their way through the bitterest cold, with scouts moving ahead to start fires where the people could warm up and rest. They ate their horses, and the weakest among them warmed their hands and feet in the carcasses of the freshly killed animals. A hundred and fifty miles to the north they came to Crazy Horse's village, where they were given food and shelter. Fourteen infants had died on the way.

From Crook's point of view, the operation was a success. His main goal always had been not to kill Indians but to strip them of their livelihood, so they would be forced onto reservations where they had to accept government support and control. The Northern Cheyenne surrendered in the spring. By mid-May, Dull Knife, Little Wolf, the two other old man chiefs, and 869 others had come in to the Red Cloud Agency in northwestern Nebraska. Crazy Horse's people surrendered about the same time.[23]

So it was that the Powder River country, including the land along the Middle Fork and its many tributaries behind the Red Wall was, in the mind of whites, cleared of Indians and mostly of buffalo by 1878. But of course things were never as simple as an account like this makes them sound—with one group of people simply succeeding the one that had been there earlier. Crow, Shoshone, Arapaho, Cheyenne and Lakota, and white, black, and mixed-race people moved through and around the Bighorns all during the 1800s. Well into the 1880s, the Shoshone, especially, turn up in various accounts camping, hunting, and visiting in a variety of places around Wyoming—including at the Bar C Ranch at the confluence of the Middle Fork and Buffalo Creek. Shoshone people camped in the meadows every summer and were well known to the cowboys and the ranch foreman, and the foreman's wife.

It was just a year after Dull Knife's surrender that a wealthy young Englishman named Moreton Frewen came to Powder River, looking for something to do with his money besides bet on cards and horses. There was plenty of grass, and no buffalo to around to eat it. It looked like a good place for a cattle empire.

# Chapter 3
## The British Come
### to
## Hole in the Wall

Before he lost his famous 76 Ranch on Powder River, Moreton Frewen's
business associates called him "Mortal Ruin."
*Courtesy American Heritage Center, University of Wyoming.*

# The Frewen Brothers

In the spring of 1878, Moreton Frewen, a young English gentleman, made his first trip to America. He was born at Northiam, a village in Sussex, in southern England, in a house his family had owned since 1583. He had no title and was not an aristocrat, but he was wealthy, a Cambridge graduate, and socialized with a fast set who spent their time gambling, hunting foxes, and pursuing love affairs in Melton Mowbray, a village in Leicestershire in central England.

Frewen came to America at the invitation of the Irish aristocrats John Adair and his wife. The Adairs promised to show him their new ranch in Palo Duro Canyon, in the Texas panhandle. On the way, In New York, Philadelphia, Washington, D.C. and Chicago, the Adairs introduced Frewen to upper-crust American society. In Chicago he met General Philip Sheridan, second in command of the U.S. Army in the West. The general extolled the big-game hunting he'd recently enjoyed in the Bighorn Mountains of Wyoming, on an expedition from Fort Washakie to the Yellowstone River. Frewen got a taste of ranching during a few weeks in Texas with the Adairs, and returned to England in July.

Frewen, twenty-five years old, had inherited a small fortune of £16,000 and was going through it briskly. That summer after a long run of good luck at cards and horses, he lost heavily in the races at Doncaster. He'd been uncertain whether to stay in England that fall or return to America and hunt big game on the Yellowstone; the losses tipped the scales. He gave his favorite thoroughbred, Redskin, to the English beauty Lillie Langtry, ending their affair at the time she was becoming the full-time mistress of the Prince of Wales. Frewen then sold the rest of his fox hunting and race horses, and sailed for New York. In Chicago this time, Sheridan advised Frewen that Indians in Montana were currently unpredictable, and he'd do better to try Wyoming. So it was that Frewen, his older brother Dick, and four other young swells got off the train at Rawlins to hunt along the North Platte and Sweetwater for two months. They ended up at Fort Washakie.

The friends returned to England for Christmas, but the Frewen brothers stayed. Jack Hargreaves, a Black Hills prospector Frewen had met in Texas, persuaded them the ranges on Powder River were worth looking at. Hargreaves guided them there, over the southern Bighorns from the Nowood River, probably by the same route Edward Rose and the Crow had led the Astorians in 1811. This time, though, it was winter; temperatures at night were down to zero. Hargreaves showed the Frewens how to round up a little buffalo herd to break trail through the snowdrifts.

Between the Tongue and Powder rivers on the east side of

the mountains, Hargreaves said, they'd find ranges nearly perfect for cattle. These ranges, he told them, were now safe for whites with the Sioux and Cheyenne more or less gone to reservations, and they would find the country unoccupied. It's still one of the great dreams of the West, the dream of unoccupied country waiting to be taken. The grass, sticking its cured, blond spears up through the snow, was so full of nutrients it could carry stock through the winter. Around Fort McKinney, near future Buffalo, there were stories of cattle abandoned in the fall that their owners had never expected to see again. Yet in spring the animals turned up, sleek and fat.[1]

His head full of schemes, Moreton headed back to England to raise money, leaving his brother Dick behind to start a ranch. Early in 1879, Moreton returned to the states. Traveling through New York, he met Clara Jerome, daughter of the millionaire Leonard Jerome. The Jerome family had recently returned from London, where Clara's sister Jennie had met and married Lord Randolph Churchill, and Jennie had given birth to their son, Winston, the future prime minister.

Out on Powder River, Moreton found Dick supervising broadax crews who were squaring up big pine logs for a house. They built it about four miles east of present Kaycee, on the north bank of Powder River a short way downstream from where the North Fork comes in. The main room, forty feet square and two stories high, could serve as a dining room or dance hall. Large fireplaces warmed the east and west ends, and a gallery for musicians ran along one side. On the ground floor were a kitchen, a pantry, and an office-library. Sleeping rooms led off the top of the carved, walnut staircase. Furniture and shingles were shipped in from Chicago, the staircase from

England. The house supposedly cost forty thousand dollars. Cowboys called it Frewen's Castle.[2]

Downstream another twenty miles was a stage stop at an abandoned army post where the old Bozeman Trail crossed Powder River. The Frewens had a store here, with a post office and, great novelty, a telephone. The line ran back to the "Ranche," as they spelled it. When guests arrived, someone was sent down promptly from the castle to escort them up.

Cowboys called Moreton and Dick Frewen's ranch house on Powder River 'Frewen's Castle,' for its luxuries and size.
*Geoffrey Millais photo, Margaret Brock Hanson collection, Hoofprints of the Past Museum.*

In the summer of 1879, Moreton and Dick bought two thousand head of cattle from a Sweetwater cowman named Tim Foley, and trailed them north to the Powder River ranges. In succeeding years the Frewens established ranches on Crazy Woman Creek, Tongue River, and far to the east on Rawhide Creek, north of Fort Laramie. With Foley's cattle had come their most famous brand, the 76, which would remain on Powder River cattle long after the Frewens had left.

Horace Plunkett, Irish aristocrat, always maintained that his years in the
Wyoming cattle business taught him far more about men than about cattle.
*Courtesy American Heritage Center, University of Wyoming.*

# Horace Plunkett

A second well-heeled British subject, Horace Plunkett, arrived on Powder River that fall of 1879 and established the NH Ranch on Beaver Creek, near present Barnum and not far north of what soon would become the famed Bar C. Unlike Frewen, Plunkett was genuine nobility; he was the third son of the 16th Baron Dunsany. With a family seat in County Meath, north of Dublin, Plunketts traced their lineage back to the 12th century and by Horace's time were among the largest landowners in Ireland. The Plunketts owned estates in England, too, and Horace was educated there, at Eton and Oxford. The troubles and future of Ireland were always close to his heart, and he would eventually make a long career there in public service, serving in the House of Commons from 1892 to 1900, advocating for cooperative systems in agriculture, and playing a central, moderate role in his country's painful split from the United Kingdom in coming decades.

Though close to the same age as the Frewens, Plunkett was more serious, more conservative, and a sharper businessman. He'd battled tuberculosis after graduating from Oxford. The disease had killed his mother and two of his siblings, and eventually would take a third. Doctors generally recommended drier climates for TB; clearly his health was part of the reason Plunkett came west. He always worried about his health, even fought for it with a kind of Teddy-Roosevelt pugnacity. He stood five feet ten but weighed only 130 pounds. He often galloped the range stripped to the waist.[3]

But why Plunkett ended up on Powder River is not clear; his diaries and letters have not survived from his first two years in Wyoming. If he and Moreton Frewen were not acquainted already, they at least had mutual friends. And even Plunkett, despite his conservative nature, was not immune to the cattle-boom fever then sweeping the British investment world.

# The Cattle Boom

In the late 1870s, reports began circulating among London, Edinburgh and Dundee capitalists that there was money to be made raising beef on the high plains of North America. In 1880, a two-man commission reported back to Parliament that an annual return of thirty-three percent on investments was ordinary. All a person had to do was establish a ranch, buy a herd, hire a few cowboys, and turn the animals loose. The grass was free and there was no need to own the land. The climate was relatively benign and the herds would increase naturally, at a predictable rate. Books, papers, and magazines quickly spread the news.

British law already made it possible for small as well as large players to buy in to companies and investment trusts. Large investors were attracted by the idea of near-feudal domains on the Plains. Management was typically delegated to hired help while the owners hosted hunting trips into the mountains and lavish parties at the "ranche." Between 1879 and 1888, thirty-three British companies registered to invest in the American ranching business. Together they raised a total capital of thirty-seven million dollars, of which twenty-seven million went directly to the United States.[4]

In Wyoming, the Anglo-American Cattle Company and the vast Swan Land and Cattle Company were both backed by British capital, with American managers. The Frewen brothers started out together in a simple partnership, while Plunkett and his partners Edward Boughton and Alexis Roche soon established a second ranch, the EK, near present Mayoworth on the North Fork of Powder River.

But soon both Plunkett and the Frewens expanded their partnerships into full-blown corporations with boards of directors and investors from across the British Isles. Frewen's Powder River Cattle Company, for example, was capitalized at £300,000, or around $1.5 million. Board chairman was the Duke of Manchester, with more nobility among the directors.[5]

# Alston and Peters

Two other investors soon joined Plunkett and the Frewens in establishing a cattle ranch on the upper Powder River. T.W. Peters was a businessman with connections in Philadelphia and England. His partner, W.C. Alston, was a Scot. Both were on Powder River in the fall of 1880, hunting and looking over the ranges. The following summer, they trailed in a herd of cattle from North Platte, Nebraska, and founded the Bar C Ranch at the confluence of Buffalo Creek and the Middle Fork of Powder River, under the cliffs of the Red Wall.

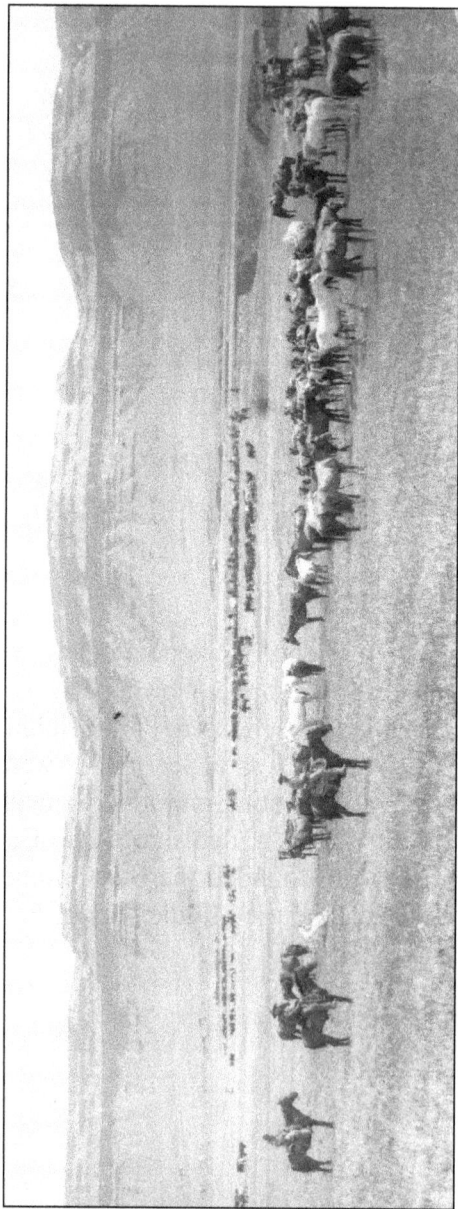

Roundup on the Bar C, about 1885, with the Red Wall in the background.
*Geoffrey Millais photo, Wold family collection.*

## Cowboys and Roundups

Because cattle grazed freely over huge expanses of country, gathering them to brand or ship was always difficult. But by the early 1880s, the Wyoming Stock Growers Association had brought some order to the business with a Territory-wide system of roundups. Wyoming was divided into districts; ranches sent one or more chuck wagons, each with a cook, a wagon boss, and a dozen or so cowboys and their mounts to the roundup of the local district. Single representatives—"reps"—were sent to the more distant roundups to collect any cattle that had wandered farther away. Routes of the roundups were published in newspapers across the Territory every April. The system was cooperative, necessary, and autocratic.

Spring roundup began in May and lasted through mid-July. Men worked up one creek, over a divide, down the

Bar C cowboys at the chuckwagon, about 1885.
*Geoffrey Millais photo, Wold family collection.*

next and so on, until, supposedly, all the cattle of the district had been gathered, the new calves branded and earmarked, and the bull calves cut. Fall roundup began in late August and ran through mid-October. At that time the calves were weaned away from their mothers, and animals to be sold that year were cut from the herd and trailed to the railroad for shipment to Chicago or Omaha for slaughter and sale.

May 1883 saw the start of one of the biggest roundups ever, when the crews gathered on Powder River at the mouth of Crazy Woman Creek. Supposedly there were four hundred cowboys on hand and fourteen hundred horses; roundup wagons were camped for two miles along the river. Fifty years later Malcolm Campbell would recall that the Frewens had eighty thousand head of cattle on their ranges that year; the EK, thirty thousand; the Bar C, nine thousand; and the NH, four thousand. These numbers are almost certainly inflated—Frewen's Powder River Cattle Company never reported more than fifty-five thousand to its investors, and even that figure would have been based on a book count, not an actual tally—but they do show the relative sizes of the different outfits.[6]

The roundup rhythms drove the cowboys' lives, with spring, summer and fall packed with work and the winters mostly idle. The men earned their forty dollars a month wages only seven or eight months a year. In winter they generally ended up "riding the grubline," as it was called. Cowboys moved from ranch to ranch and were welcomed, fed, and bunked as long as they didn't stay too long, helped with chores, and brought useful news, gossip, songs, poems or stories. They were proud of their skills with horses, cattle, and firearms. Many dressed carefully and elaborately, and liked to spend money on silver trim for themselves and their horses. Lore and the prejudices of a distant press made all cowboys out to be profligates, spending their wages as soon as they got to town, shooting up whorehouses and pool halls in boyish glee. Surely some were frugal and some were not; some had a permanent itch to drift, while others planned carefully for futures that included livestock, land, and families of their own.

The more skilled and intelligent cowboys rose to be wagon bosses, or even foremen; these are the men whose names and reputations survived them. Nate Champion and Jack Flagg, for example, who were to play such prominent roles on the rustler side when Johnson County was invaded in 1892, were both Bar C wagon bosses at different times. The foremen—E.W. Murphy and Fred Hesse on the 76, Jack Donoghue, Johnny Pierce and Mike Shonsey on the NH and the EK, Hank Devoe on the Bar C—were the true barons of the range, the local leaders who actually ran the ranches on a daily basis, year round.

# The Swells

The British ranch owners' lives swung even more drastically with the seasons. As a rule they spent summers in Wyoming and winters back home. Summers they often worked right along with the roundups; Plunkett, at least, certainly did. Plunkett also traveled to the stockyards with the cattle to oversee their sale, poking the animals with a goad at every stop to make sure none of the animals had gone down in the cattle cars, and then scampering back to the caboose along the top of the train once it started up again. From the stockyards he continued by train to New York, and by steamship home to Ireland.

Frewen, similarly, later claimed to have crossed the Atlantic one hundred times in the short decade he was connected with the business. Plunkett, who always seemed to take his family responsibilities more seriously than Frewen did,

An English guest of the Bar C Ranch, in full hunting gear.
*Geoffrey Millais photo, mid 1880s, Wold family collection.*

was generally glad to get back to Ireland and its seasonal round of fox hunts, race balls, family obligations, and business.

During the summer and fall the foreigners welcomed a steady stream of guests, English and American—including Frewen's bride, Clara Jerome Frewen, who came to Powder River only once.[7] These swells are the ones captured in the cowboys' stories, blurting "yoicks!" at the cattle as though they were hounds, or asking a foreman if his "mahster" was at home, and receiving the answer, "the son of a bitch hasn't been born yet."[8]

T.W. Peters became known among the cowboys as "Twice Wintered" Peters, for staying two winters in Wyoming. Much of that time he was in Cheyenne; by 1885 he and his wife lived in a house at Seventeenth and Russell streets. He was on the executive committee of the Stock Growers Association, was often present at their monthly meetings, and in 1886 ran unsuccessfully for the Territorial Council—the senate—as a representative of Cheyenne's Laramie County. Alston's whereabouts are harder to pin down; he seems to have continued making trips across the Atlantic.[9]

Alston and Peters were both on Powder River in the fall of 1880, when a Major Lewis Wise, on his way around the world from England by way of the Suez Canal, Australia, and San Francisco, stopped at the Frewens' ranch for a big-game hunt in the Bighorns. Wise, Alston, and an Australian named Frank Boughton each had a local hunter assigned to them. The hunters guided them to game and probably did much of the skinning and dressing out of the heads. With a cook and a wrangler, the party came to eight men, eighteen horses, three mules, and a dog.

They were in the mountains for seven weeks. They went up the Beaver Creek drainage, and then hunted the headwaters of the Red, North, and Middle forks of Powder River. They made it over to the western slope once or twice, and finally came out down Sheep Creek to where it meets the Middle Fork on what soon would become the Bar C. Wise kept a good journal of the hunt, and at the end carefully charted each of the kills. These were mostly big game, except for five wolves and two foxes killed by the wrangler. The total bag was sixty-four head. Alston killed thirteen, including four elk, two bison, and a "Cinnamon bear." Boughton killed ten animals, and Wise twenty-three, including nine elk, two grizzlies, and two bison. The bison and some of the mule deer were generally used for bear bait. The bear hunts were, of course, the most exciting. Wise's guide, Oliver P. Hanna was mauled when he followed a wounded bear into a thicket. But no bones were broken, and according to Wise, Hanna recovered in just two weeks, thanks to the major's willingness to change the bandages three times daily.

They arrived back at Frewen's Castle on October 22, the same day as Lords Caledon and Rodney, two other aristocrats who'd been hunting in the mountains at the same time. Alston and Moreton Frewen rode off to Crazy Woman Creek for a day or two to check on the cattle operations there, as "Alston has some thoughts of investing," Wise wrote. A night or two later, Peters, whom Wise called "a young Ranche-man," stopped in for a visit. "He had a very good voice," Wise remembered, "and we had a pleasant evening with some good songs."[10]

# The Bar C

The summer after the successful hunting trip, Alston and Peters, as we have seen, brought in cattle from Nebraska and founded the Bar C. They built a house that, like Frewens', was made of big, squared logs. Though it was only one storey, photos show two chimneys, and supposedly there were four fireplaces attached to each. There was a barn, and various outbuildings.

They hired Hank Devoe as foreman. Hank and his wife May made the Bar C a center of domestic and social life west of the Red Wall in the 1880s. With his father and brothers Hank had come to the Territory from Marysville, Kansas, and freighted from the Union Pacific Railroad at Rock Creek to Fort Fetterman, near present Douglas on the North Platte.

Hank and May by 1878 were living in a cabin at the base of the mountain above Fort McKinney (present Buffalo), where

The Bar C ranch house, about 1885.
The buffalo-jump bluff is visible on the right edge of the picture, and the low barn in the background.
*Geoffrey Millais photo, Wold family collection.*

he hauled wood for the Army. Hank was a tall, well-built man with a square jaw, thick moustache, and expressive eyes. A photo of him survives, standing in front of the ranch house, with an elbow on his saddled horse, wearing cartridge belt, pistol, tall boots, spurs, trousers with an extra layer of leather inside the legs, hat, shirt, and necktie.

Hank Devoe was the first foreman of the Bar C.
*Geoffrey Millais photo, Wold family collection.*

The Devoes at the Bar C barn about 1885.
Left to right: Hank Devoe, unknown ranch hand, Earl Devoe,
Liddy Devoe in the arms of her mother, May.
*Geoffrey Millais photo, Margaret Brock Hanson collection, Hoofprints of the Past Museum.*

A blurred photo of May with a child in her arms survives as well. She was remembered as a plain-looking, lively, capable, sensible woman, who made funny faces and made friends easily among Indians and whites. She was also a skilled healer, riding wherever she was needed, sidesaddle on her bay mare, carrying her black satchel.

One fall a chief of one of the Indian bands that still hunted every year on the Middle Fork came to May to say his daughter was sick with a high fever. She was able to help the young woman get better over the next two weeks. Then one wet day when the snows had melted the following spring, the woman and several of her Indian friends returned, bringing a yard of calico and a big spoon, as thanks. But "on this trip she took cold," May remembered years later, "had double pneumonia and this time I could not save her."

Shoshone and Arapaho Indians would camp along the Middle Fork during late fall and winter in bands of four or five hundred people to hunt buffalo, dry meat for their own use, and tan hides for sale. May Devoe grew close to several of the Indian women, and for many years told the story of how they once avoided disaster after some whites had brought whiskey into the Indian camp. Hank was away. May was deeply worried until one of the women came quietly to her door, to say the women in camp had tied the passed-out whites and Indians together with rawhide thongs, as the men slept off the celebration.

Hank Devoe and Fred G.S. Hesse, foreman of the 76 outfit, had the mail contract for the route from the old Bozeman Trail's Powder River crossing to the Bar C. May acted as postmistress at the ranch house. From the Bar C the mail was hauled over the mountain, almost certainly by the same old Indian routes taken by the westbound Astorians, and later by the eastbound Frewens following buffalo through the snowdrifts. This was horseback mail, at least at first; a rider went down to Powder River Crossing one day and back the next, twice a week.[11]

There's no doubt the Devoes made the ranch a lively place. Stories came down through the years of dances at the Bar C where cleaned-up, gleaming cowboys danced with titled ladies, to the delight of both sides.[12]

Hank had strong feelings for May, but of course disguised them. A story circulated for years of an English guest, who one day went hunting above the Bar C. Later, a big cougar came up out of the creek bed and headed for the house. Just as the cat leapt through the open kitchen window, the hunter reappeared. Over by a corral post, Hank was lazily lighting his pipe. Some racket came from the kitchen, but Hank puffed quietly on.

Finally the Brit could hold it in no longer. "My God, man! Isn't your wife in there?"

"Reckon she is," Hank replied.

Brit: "Aren't you going to do something?"

Hank: "Hell, man—we've got no use for them pesky critters and danged if *I'm* going to help him out. Let him get out of there as best he can."[13]

One of those Englishmen, perhaps the one in the story, was Geoffrey Millais, son of John Millais, the pre-Raphaelite painter and one of the best-known artists in England at the time. By the 1880s, John Millais was earning £30,000 a year for his portraits of England's cabinet ministers, actresses, and aristocrats. Geoffrey Millais invested heavily with Alston and Peters, but unlike most other partners and investors, he spent three summers on the ranch, wrote letters home to his parents and an uncle, and took some splendid glass-negative photos—the portrait of Hank Devoe is a good example.

Roundup found young Geoffrey sometimes in the saddle eighteen hours at a time. When a pair of horses decided to head for Utah, he chased them 250 miles before catching them. He took a photo of an Indian, whom he persuaded to pose in return for a meal and a cup of coffee. He looked forward to the arrival of his brother, Johnnie, and had found a hunter for him named Rattlesnake Jack.[14] He was smitten by the look of the country:

*In the photos I am sending you will see a great deal of rock which in nature is a deep red color. The sun*

Steamboat Rock, near the Bar C Ranch headquarters.
Geoffrey Millais photo, about 1885.
*Margaret Brock Hanson collection, Hoofprints of the Past Museum.*

*setting on these rocks is a wonderful sight...These rocks are hundreds of feet high in places. The cattle feed all along the foot of them, which you will see in the photos, forms a valley. The mountains rise on the other side. You might show [the photos] to the family. I hope it will give you some idea of the country I am in as it is unlike anything one sees in Europe or Eastern America. They are about the first taken in this part of America.*[15]

Geoffrey was wrapped up in dreams of profit, at least the first summer in Wyoming. "Our cattle are looking very well indeed in fact fatter than any other lot in the country," he wrote his mother in August 1884. He had invested £5300, about $16,000, with Peters and Alston sometime the year before. In that first year, he was confident, the value of his investment had already grown by £1500—a tidy 28%—"which shows what a good business it is," he wrote. He was equally confident his stake would continue growing, despite the fact that he expected only £200 that fall as his share of the beef sales, which would mean a real return on his investment of only 3.7 percent.[16]

Already by 1884, the cattle business was softening. Prices had peaked in the late fall of 1882; those prices brought floods of investors with floods of cattle. The limit on the prosperity turned out to be the range itself. In the late seventies and early eighties, one unusually wet year followed another; for a time, it seemed as if the range's carrying capacity was as expansive as its horizons. Then more normal weather returned with the winter of 1884-85. Calf crops were down that spring, and fall roundup produced skinny beeves. There were now around two million cattle in Wyoming, four times as many as in 1880. Ranchers shipped greater numbers of steers to try and recoup earlier losses. But the animals were weakened by the hard winter and scant grass, and prices continued to spiral downward.

# The Boom Collapses

Years later, Moreton Frewen's investors would nickname him "Mortal Ruin," for the way he charged disastrously through other people's money. In 1882, Moreton decided it was time to buy out his brother Dick. To do so he expanded their earlier partnership into a corporation, the Powder River Cattle Company, Ltd., and sold £300,000 (about $1.5 million) in common and preferred stock in a week. Board chairman was the Duke of Manchester; directors included the Earl of Wharncliffe and Sir Henry Nevill.[17]

The Frewens sold all their Wyoming holdings to the company. In return, Moreton kept one-third of the shares, and agreed to manage the company for five years at no salary. Instead he would receive a third of the profits remaining each year after a ten percent dividend had been paid to all other investors. It looked, of course, like a sure thing; Moreton's original letter to potential investors (there was nothing so formal as a prospectus) implied that he and Dick, between the rise in value of the herds and what they'd taken out of the business, had shown returns near sixty percent for the first two years. By September 1882, Moreton had used one million dollars of the fresh cash to buy more cattle. By the book count, he now had forty thousand head.[18]

Confident prices would keep rising, Frewen contracted with his neighbor Horace Plunkett to buy EK cattle at an even higher price a year later. When the fall of 1883 came, Plunkett found Frewen's price guaranteed him a tidy six dollars per head more than he could get in Chicago. Frewen at first notified Plunkett the contract had been repudiated; Plunkett refused to comply, and the two looked to their neighbors on the Bar C to help them out of their disagreement. Alston would serve as Plunkett's arbitrator, and Peters as Frewen's. Frewen was satisfied as he figured any payments under the arbitration wouldn't be due for two years anyway, and Plunkett figured he'd made an extra six thousand dollars when he sold his cattle in Chicago.[19]

Still, Frewen kept expanding the company. He set up a feeding operation in Superior, Wisconsin. He negotiated for summer range in Alberta. He set up a refrigeration plant at Sherman, on top of the hill between Laramie and Cheyenne. Dividends dwindled. Stock prices fell.

In the spring of 1885, to save expenses and to smooth out roughening relations with his board, Frewen came up with the idea of naming an outside manager at £1,000 per year. Frewen would pay the salary from his own pocket for the balance of the five years on his original contract with the directors. He offered the job to Plunkett, who declined, pleading poor health. He offered it next to T. W. Peters, who accepted. Trying to get control of an operation that seemed to be expanding in all directions at once, Peters told the board the operation in Superior was a failure, and the Alberta lease a bad idea. But Peters ran into resistance in Wyoming, where one of the 76 foremen, F. W. Murphy, countered that he was sure the Superior operation could make a thirty or forty thousand dollar profit—and told the board so, himself.

Meanwhile, the overstocked range was getting worse. Ranchers were driving stock into the mountains to look for grass. Fred Hesse, the other 76 foreman, estimated the company loss the previous winter had been fifteen percent, with the calf brand down by a thousand from the previous year.

Then, Murphy sent a company herd north to new range in Montana. Hesse was there to count them on arrival, and the tally came up short by a thousand head. Peters fired Murphy. Discontent with Peters began to spread on the range. Frewen had his own sources of Wyoming information and kept his hand in, stirring the pot.

In November, Frewen demanded that the board end its arrangement with Peters the following summer. Frewen argued for winter feeding, and for selling off some of the breeding stock to pay for the feeding operation—which would have meant moving some of the breeding stock all the way to Alberta, where there was grass. Peters opposed both ideas. Moreton said he'd be willing again to take over from Peters the following year; Peters opposed that idea, too. Finally, the board backed Peters, and Moreton Frewen sued.[20]

The board was now in turmoil, and at a bitter shareholders' meeting in London in February 1886, charges and countercharges flew. These were, after all, investors who had come into the business expecting annual dividends of twenty-five to forty percent, scrambling now to recoup even a fraction of their initial investments. Peters was at the London meeting to argue against moving cattle off the Powder River ranges, and finally threatening to leave the company if it closed down its offices in Cheyenne. The shareholders elected a new board, voted Moreton Frewen onto the board (he'd been only manager since the company was formed), and gave another seat to a third brother, Ted Frewen. The board then gave a new committee two weeks to investigate policies and management— and it came down on Frewen's side of the arguments: the feeding operation could work; moving cattle to Alberta might take pressure off the range, too. Finally, the new board offered the managership to Plunkett. He took the job in March 1886. Frewen promised not to meddle, but he was a natural meddler. And Peters was glad to retire from the fray.[21]

The winter of 1885-1886 was mild, the best since 1877-1878, Fred Hesse reported, and the cattle came through it pretty well. Still, the ranges were overstocked, meaning prices would stay low, and railroad rates were continuing to rise. So it's not surprising that when spring roundup began, the Stock Growers Association moved to cut wages. When Plunkett arrived back in Wyoming, manager now both of his own operations and of the Powder River Cattle Company's, he found his cowboys believed him to be responsible for the wage cut.

"They have been talking of shooting me all winter, as I have been made the scapegoat of the attempt to reduce wages," he wrote en route to roundup. " I think I shall outlive it. But it is unpleasant being scowled at by blackguards."[22]

On roundup on the South Fork of Powder River—this

The Bar C Roundup Crew, about 1884. Standing, left to right: Hank Devoe, Ray Peters (probably T.W. Peters or a relative), George Gordon, Chester Morris, Nate Champion, Joe Vincent. Seated, left to right: Buck Jackson, unknown, Mr. Hall (this may be the builder of the Hall Cabin at the mouth of Outlaw Canyon), unknown, unknown, Al Allison, Bill Rankin, Jack Flagg.) Flagg was one of the ringleaders of the strike on the 1886 roundup, and many of these men would have sympathized with the strikers.

*Courtesy of the Johnson County Jim Gatchell Museum.*

would include wagons from the NH, EK, Bar C, and 76 outfits, plus a few small neighbors and reps from more distant ranches—the cowboys refused to work until wages were boosted back to forty dollars. Men already making forty dollars didn't want to work alongside others making thirty-five and thirty dollars a month. "Not a wheel moved," the *Rocky Mountain Husbandman* reported, until the foremen would submit to the cowboys' demand. Finally, the foremen submitted, and the reps were sent back to their ranches with the same demand. Only the reps from the huge Carey ranches down on the North Platte—the SO and the CY—came back with a negative answer. The cowboys on Powder River refused to let them on the roundup, and the CY cattle went unworked and the calves unbranded.

The strike spread quickly to roundups on the North Platte and on the Sweetwater. It might be hard to believe that cowboys, proud then as now of their individualism, would ever do anything requiring group action. But it did happen. They may have been influenced by the Knights of Labor, who recently had won a strike against the Union Pacific Railroad and who may have been recruiting Texas and Wyoming cowboys. But there is no proof of this. It is clear, however, that the strike began to spread. Economic uncertainties were driving a wedge between employers and employees that would widen into bloodshed in the feuds of 1891 and 1892—the so-called Johnson County War. In Cheyenne, Thomas Sturgis, secretary of the Stock Growers, decided to press criminal breach-of-peace charges against the strikers. But none of the CY cowboys would testify. So Sturgis came up with the idea of a blacklist.[23]

Peters, who was a member of the Stock Growers Association's executive committee, was not on hand at a meeting July 20, 1886, when the committee authorized Sturgis to "prepare and issue a circular" giving the names of "the ring leaders in the 'mutiny' on round up No. #23 on the 'Black list'" and "stating the reasons for placing said names on the 'Black List,' to all the men in the Territory." The blackballing, that is, would be public, and permanent, and Territory-wide.

Peters did show up at the next meeting, August 2, when the committee decided not to publish the circular after all, until more information could be obtained and a larger representation of the committee was on hand.

Peters persuaded them it would be unwise to make martyrs of the strikers. He threatened to resign from the committee, and refused specifically to fire Jack Flagg, who had been repping for the Bar C on one of the more southern roundups, and agitating for a strike. Were it not for Peters, the association could well have taken a harder line, and the strike could have spread and become violent. After that, the record fades.[24]

The Territory soon had a far worse disaster on its hands. It began to snow.

The losses of the terrible winter of 1886-1887 were enormous, and the winter itself is often blamed for the end of the cattle boom. But the end was already underway; the bust had already begun. That terrible winter—snow deep enough to bury the fence posts, followed by a January thaw and re-freeze that left the Plains a sheet of ice, cattle piling up in gullies and dying by the thousands—was simply the death blow to an industry already staggering on wobbling legs.

Not until the following July were the losses fully apparent. The Powder River Cattle Company reported herd losses at seventy-five percent. Frewen took a temporary job as a sort of fixer for Sir Salar Jung, until recently the prime minister for the Nizam of Hyderabad, of India. Plunkett was able to turn an enormous financial mess at the Powder River Cattle Company into a more or less orderly retreat. He began to liquidate his own holdings at the same time, and on his way out of Wyoming was given some praise and speeches at the Cheyenne Club that left him feeling better about the West.[25] He returned to Ireland to help his ailing father, but returned to Wyoming again in the spring of 1888 to tie up loose ends. That fall he returned to Ireland to live, and pursue one of the most remarkable careers ever in Irish politics and agriculture. Always afterward, he maintained that he'd learned a great deal more in Wyoming about men than about cattle.

Alston ended up in Cheyenne without enough money to get back to England. Peters was rumored to be drinking. His wife was by this time running a boardinghouse in Cheyenne. Plunkett gave a dinner for a group of Cheyenne Britons, partly to provide some business for her and thereby help the family. In the fall of 1890, the Peterses sold their Cheyenne house on 17th and Russell streets, for $8,400.[26]

The Bar C folded as a Peters-Alston operation by 1889. By 1891, there were only two wagons on the Powder River roundup. Johnny Pierce, the one foreman Plunkett had gotten along with, was bossing the 76. Mike Shonsey, another former Plunkett foreman, was in charge of what remained of the EK and NH herds. The Bar C cattle had been folded in with these.

At the Bar C, a man named Tommy Carr was running things for Shonsey, and soon filed a land claim there in his own name. And from a cabin half a mile away, at the mouth of the Middle Fork canyon, a man well known behind the Red Wall as a top hand and former Bar C wagon boss was running a small herd of his own. Just a couple of hundred head in the old Bar C pastures. His reputation was clear: he was honest, soft spoken, laconic, and quick with a pistol.

His name was Nate Champion.

# Chapter 4
## Rustler Heaven

# A HISTORY

The spring of 1891 was a good one on Powder River. Overstocking had ended; the range and the cattle had largely recovered from the disasters of four years before. Those disasters had driven out the best known of the previous owners—the Frewens, Plunkett, Alston and Peters—but the remnants of their outfits were still in the hands of distant owners, who left local decisions up to their managers and foremen.

At the same time, the country had begun to be homesteaded by smaller owners, many with families, running a few cows of their own and often working for wages at the same time. "Ben this country has changed a heap," Nate Champion wrote his brother that March; "grangers on every creek nearly all of them has got a few cattle[.] I dont know what I will do this summer. I have got a few cattle and I dont know whether I will work for any of these out fits or not."

The collapse had thrown a lot of cowboys out of work, but many had stayed. These were the "grangers" he mentions. They were small businessmen where before there had been only management and labor, that is, ranch foremen and cowboys. Now, these grangers were making decisions of their own: where

to run their cattle, how many to run. The land was still largely
unclaimed and unfenced. The grass was still free. But there
remained an older network of custom about who got to use what
grass, and what water. Simply to make a living, grangers like
Nate were bound to shake things up.

Rustlers, they were also called. Mostly the word meant
someone good at rustling up solutions to all kinds of problems.
If that included occasionally burning his own brand on a calf
that had slipped unbranded through the roundup, well, so be it.
"Rustler" wasn't necessarily a pejorative term. Champion would
have accepted it for himself. And like any true rustler, he would
have felt contempt for a common cow thief.[1]

# Nate Champion

Born in Williamson County, Texas, in 1857, Champion probably came north with a trail herd and by 1882 was working for Plunkett on the EK. By 1884 he was a wagon boss on the Bar C, in charge of one of the roundup crews. In 1886 he was a wagon boss on the EK; Plunkett at the end of the season noted in his diary he was sorry to see Champion go; he was "a good man." In 1888 he was again back with the EK. When the EK foreman was fired near the end of that season, three cowboys went with him. Probably Champion was one of them.

Among his neighbors, Champion had a reputation for honesty. A story is told in the Brock family, who ranched on the North Fork of Powder River, of Nate's once looking after the ranch while the family was away. When Albert Brock got home, he joined Champion for a meal; Nate apologized for the lack of potatoes. Brock noted there were plenty in the root

Nate Champion wrote his brother in the spring of 1891 that there were
"grangers on every creek" in the Hole-in-the-Wall Country,
and he was hoping soon to get a place of his own.
*Courtesy of the Johnson County Jim Gatchell Museum.*

cellar. Didn't Nate know that? "Yes," was the reply. "But they weren't mine."

When Nate wrote his brother again in April 1891, he was staying "on Red Fork where the old Sioux Trail crosses,"—site of the present Brock Hanson ranch. (Brock Hanson is a great grandson of Albert Brock.)

Nate and a partner, Ross Gilbertson, had 140 head of cattle and eight saddle horses. Gilbertson was working for wages on one of the bigger ranches while Nate looked after the stock. Champion noted to his brother that he was out of debt, and that the future looked good: "if a man wants to take a ranch he can make a grub stake [working for wages] in the summer and improve his ranch in the winter. I haven't got any ranch but I think I will take one this spring…think I will move up to big valley in a few days." By "big valley" he meant the valley west of the Red Wall. Apparently, his plans were to turn his cattle loose in the Bar C pasture.[2]

# Owen Wister
# Through the Bar C Gap

Nate posted those letters from the Mayoworth Post Office, on the North Fork, near the old EK headquarters. Post offices then were social centers; people rode long distances for mail, understanding that on arrival, they might have to wait an extra day or two for the mail carrier to arrive. The Bar C headquarters, as noted earlier, was a post office in the mid-1880s. By 1891 that function had moved unofficially to the Blue Creek Ranch, known also as the Riverside post office, northwest of the Bar C and west of Barnum.[3]

In June 1891 a local rancher, Bob Tisdale, came for his mail, accompanied by a visitor from Philadelphia. Owen Wister would become author of *The Virginian*, the millions-selling novel that would establish the cowboy permanently as a good guy in the American imagination. Wister was on the lookout for stories.

The Tisdale brothers' TTT ranch lay about ten miles east of the Red Wall, near where Willow Creek joins the South Fork of Powder River. Wister arrived at Tisdales' on June 12, after a sixty-five mile buggy ride from Casper, looking forward to seeing a friend named Morris, a partner of the Tisdales who was away on roundup. Four days later, Bob Tisdale and Wister rode the twenty miles northwest to Riverside, by way of the Bar C Gap, a relatively easy route through the Red Wall just east of the Bar C headquarters. At Riverside they slept on the bunkhouse floor one night, not wanting to fight the bedbugs, and spent a second night outside. Also on hand was Henry Smith, "the only unabridged 'bad man' I have ever had a chance to know," Wister wrote in his diary, and model for some of his later villains. Late the second night the mail arrived, having been delayed by high water in the creeks. Next morning Tisdale did some horse trading, after which he and Wister left, taking with them the mail for the men at the Tisdale ranch.

Now they were leading two more horses, one of them a big, bucking sorrel that Tisdale planned to make into a team horse. "We came along comfortably by the Carrs' ranch on Middle Fork,"—Tommy Carr was then holding down the Bar C—passing three vultures on a high bluff "with wings spread out to catch the sun," Wister wrote.

As they headed back up through the Bar C gap, Tisdale roped the two new horses together, and began driving them in front. The big sorrel dashed up a steep slope onto the red ridges above, dragging the other horse with him. Then, while Tisdale was on foot closing a gate, his saddle horse stepped on its rein and would not budge. In a fury, Tisdale dug his boot heel into the horse's foot, just above the hoof, and began kicking the animal; when it finally lifted its foot Tisdale heel-gouged the other foot as well, swearing loudly. Then he remounted, and soon exhausted his own horse, charging after the two fleeing horses up steep slopes and down. When his horse could move no longer Tisdale began beating it badly, and finally gouged out its left eye.

They never did catch the other two horses. Wister, sickened by the deed and sickened, too, by his own failure to speak up, followed along silently and, before his friend Morris turned up, spent two more bleak days back at the ranch. During that time, watching his host down by the river beating another horse with a fence post, Wister learned from the cook that Tisdale was well known for cruelty to his animals, that the two hundred men who'd worked for him over the years all spoke of it.[4]

What Wister didn't know was that, not long before, Tisdale had suffered a public humiliation, which almost certainly was still in his heart as he abused his horse. The man who had humiliated him was Nate Champion.

# The Champion-Tisdale Feud

In 1891 Bob Tisdale and his brother John N. had turned two thousand head of cattle into the Buffalo Creek valley—the old Bar C pasture, more or less vacant now, and lush with grass. When Champion turned his little herd in there as well, Tisdale went ballistic.

Honest Nate appears not to have had so honest a reputation among big owners like the Tisdales. Champion was good friends with Jack Flagg, who had been blackballed from the Powder River Roundup ever since the strike of 1886. Flagg and four friends had started the Hat Ranch on the North Fork of the Powder, and the Hat ran separate roundups of its own. Since that time, Champion had continued to work for the EK, one of the big outfits. But when Champion wrote his brother that he was tending the stock while Gilbertson worked for wages, Nate didn't add that working for himself was his only option. Like Flagg, he, too, had been blackballed.

There had been friction. EK Foreman Mike Shonsey had promised Champion to do the neighborly thing and cut out a handful of Nate's cattle that had mixed in with a larger EK bunch. But then Shonsey went a step further, directing his cowboys to scatter Champion's little bunch after they'd been cut out. Nate had public words with Shonsey over this. Events like these went unforgotten.

Whether the Tisdales thought the Bar C pasture was too far from their home ranch, or didn't want trouble with Champion and his friends is unclear. They drove their cattle back out of there—but took some Champion cattle with them.

Confrontation came when the official Powder River roundup for 1891 was on the South Fork, home country for the Tisdales. One night the roundup found itself across the river from a so-called "independent" roundup of Champion and his friends. The next morning, Tisdale's men started riding in their wide circle and before noon had gathered fifteen hundred cattle. They pushed the stock back to within a mile of their camp. Their horses by then were tired and the men most likely were, too.

At that point Champion's men rode up, all of them armed, on fresh mounts. They cut out the calves and scattered the rest of the herd. By then it was near dark; the next morning they branded the calves, and then left. There was little the Tisdales could do. And that fact, one historian has suggested, shows as much about the shallow support for Tisdale among his own men, as it does about Champion's boldness. It was another public confrontation, and it only left more unsettled scores.[5]

# The Attack On Champion

By fall, Champion and Ross Gilbertson were living in a tiny cabin they rented from W.H. Hall, at the mouth of the Middle Fork canyon a mile or so above the old Bar C headquarters.[6] On the morning of November 1, as the best-known version of the story goes, Nate and Ross were asleep on the bunk when their door was shoved open and three armed men sprang into the cabin. "We've got you," they said; "You may as well give up."

Nonchalantly stretching and yawning, Champion reached for his holstered six-shooter on the bedpost. One of the attackers fired first, the gun so close that powder burned Champion's face. But the bullet went into the pillow; Champion fired almost simultaneously, but missed. A second shot from the attackers went into the bed. Then the three men ran off. Champion shot after them through the now-closed door at about belt height, and when he got to where he could see outside, he saw one of the attackers running crouched over, perhaps wounded. The man made his way into the thick brush along the river.

The attackers had left two Winchesters, one by the door and a second leaning against the woodpile. When Nate stepped out to get the closer one, a man appeared around the corner of the cabin with a leveled pistol. This, Nate would later testify, was Newcastle-based stock detective Joe Elliott. Nate then jumped back into the cabin, stuck the rifle through the chinking, fired again, and the man ran off.

About seventy-five yards away, Champion and Gilbertson found four overcoats and other personal stuff, left by the

The Hall cabin, where Nate Champion and Ross Gilbertson were attacked by detectives in the fall of 1891.
*Courtesy of the Johnson County Jim Gatchell Museum.*

attackers. Champion made his way on foot down to the Bar C buildings. Tommy Carr was milking a cow in the barn, and for the rest of his life remembered the feeling he suddenly got that someone was looking at him. He turned around and there was Nate, Winchester in hand, asking if Tommy had seen anyone that morning.

Champion and Gilbertson followed the attackers' trail north past what's now Barnum until they found a campsite near the old NH headquarters on Beaver Creek, where foreman Mike Shonsey now lived, running the remnants of the NH, EK, and Bar C ranches. The campsite had been abandoned in a hurry. The campers had left behind a tarpaulin soaked in blood. In the minds of the rustlers at least, two things were clear— one of Champion's shots had done some damage, and Shonsey was involved.

But other versions have made their way down through time as well. Casper resident Colin Taylor's great-great-uncle Jim Stubbs had the first land patent on the Blue Creek Ranch, taken up about this time. The story that came down through Stubbses and Taylors is that Mike Shonsey visited Champion and Gilbertson the night before, ostensibly to talk about a horse trade. Afterward, Champion suspected something was up. Early next morning, he'd heard a noise in the corral and sent Gilbertson out for a look. Gilbertson never came back and Champion, wide awake and armed, was waiting in the cabin's darkest corner when the attackers burst in. Who shot first is anyone's guess, and whether Gilbertson might have been a spy for the attackers is an open question.[7]

And then there was the story the ninety-four year old ex-shotgun man on the Barnum stage told archeologist Glenn Sweem, in 1960, the summer Sweem was excavating the floor of the petroglyph cave a few miles up the Middle Fork from the

Bar C. The old man recalled that fall of 1891—vividly. He'd met four men on the road near Barnum the morning Champion was attacked. They were leading a fifth horse with a dead man slung over the saddle.[8]

After the attack on Champion, the crimes continued. Champion's friend, John A. Tisdale, ranching then on Red Fork (and no relation to Bob and John N. Tisdale of the TTT), was murdered from ambush Dec. 1, 1891. Their friend Orley Jones was murdered a few days before that, though his body was not found until shortly after Tisdale's murder.

That winter, the grangers in Johnson County formed an association of their own: the Northern Wyoming Farmers' and Stockgrowers' Association. They announced their plans of a separate roundup—the rustlers' roundup—to begin May 1, ahead of the official, Wyoming Stock Growers Association roundup.

But it never happened. On April 5, about twenty-five of the state's largest ranch owners and twenty-five Texas gunmen they'd hired traveled north from Cheyenne to Casper on a special train, and continued north on horseback to Johnson County. They had a list, supposedly, of seventy rustlers they planned to kill. Champion's name was said to top the list.

# The Invasion

The Invasion of Johnson County, also called "the Johnson County War" or "the War on Powder River," was murderous in intent, incompetent in leadership, and ambiguous in outcome. Its leaders, supposedly convinced no rustlers would ever be convicted in Johnson County, felt compelled to take vigilante action. The leaders were Frank Wolcott, manager of the VR Ranch on Deer Creek in Converse County, and Frank Canton, a detective and former sheriff of Johnson County. Other ranchers included Bob and John N. Tisdale; other hired men included Mike Shonsey and such well-known stock detectives as Joe Elliott and Phil DuFran. The twenty-five Texans, many of them range detectives and former peace officers, were recruited around Paris, Texas, by the Texan Tom Smith, and were paid by the ranchers.

The invaders were delayed from the start by bad

weather—spitting snow and April mud. They stopped at Tisdales' to let their wagons catch up, and were told Champion—the Tisdales' old enemy—and a dozen other rustlers were staying at the KC Ranch. The next day the invaders found only two rustlers there, and killed them both—Champion and his friend Nick Ray. Though telegraph wires had been cut, word got out thanks to Jack Flagg. Flagg happened by KC in a buckboard with his stepson, Alonzo, en route to the state Democratic convention.

The invaders, besieging a cabin with Champion and a dying Ray inside it, fired on Flagg and the boy, but they escaped—back to Buffalo. There they spread the alarm. The invaders forted up at the TA Ranch south of Buffalo, where they were soon surrounded by two or three hundred armed citizens deputized by Johnson County Sheriff Red Angus. The siege lasted two days. Finally the rustlers built a movable log fort on two wagons' running gear, and were approaching the ranch buildings for a final showdown, with dynamite, when the cavalry arrived from Fort McKinney. The invaders were arrested and taken back to Cheyenne under military guard. All were charged with murder, but their defense, led by future U.S. Supreme Court Justice Willis VanDevanter, was skillful at delay. Before there was a trial, Johnson County ran out of money to prosecute the case and charges were dropped.[9]

Less well known are some crimes that came in the wake of the Invasion. In May, three members of the Red Sash Gang—the worst element of the rustler community—murdered George Wellman, the well-liked foreman of the Hoe Ranch on lower Powder River. Wellman's sympathies were probably with the invaders, and he was serving temporarily as a deputy U.S. marshal when he was killed. Johnson County officials, filled with rustler sympathy that year, failed to prosecute anyone.

Henry Smith, whom Wister had met at the Riverside post office, was almost certainly one of the murderers.

The invaders, meanwhile, pressed for a declaration of martial law in Wyoming. They didn't get it, but in June a troop of buffalo soldiers from the Ninth Cavalry at Fort Robinson in northwest Nebraska was sent to show the flag on Powder River. The troops camped outside Suggs, a vice town at the end of tracks on the Burlington railroad line then building northwest from Gillette. Something like a race riot erupted in the town after some off-duty soldiers visited one day, and one of the soldiers was killed. The event may have been provoked by sympathizers with the invaders.

And finally, in the spring of 1893, Dudley Champion, Nate's brother, confronted Mike Shonsey on the old Horseshoe Ranch near Manville. Shonsey shot him dead, and then rode sixty miles to Douglas to turn himself in to the Converse County Sheriff. The killing was ruled self defense. [10]

As for Jack Flagg, he bought a newspaper. Flagg was educated, a former schoolteacher, born and raised in West Virginia and tempered in Texas. The articles he contributed to the Buffalo *Bulletin* the summer after the invasion are, though colored by his biases, still the most ambitious and thorough contemporary accounts of those events. The following year he bought the *Bulletin's* competitor, the Buffalo *Echo*, changed its name to *The People's Voice*, and for five years made himself a voice for grangers and their families who looked for egalitarian, material progress. Where Wister and his friend the artist Frederic Remington nostalgically mourned the loss of the open spaces of the West, Flagg and people like him were eager to see it filling up—with people and economic opportunities.[11]

# Butch and Sundance

But for a while longer, the country on the headwaters of the Middle Fork maintained a kind of wary neutrality toward people on the run from the law. This was understandable, given the events of 1892, when the law had been so blatantly stolen by the powerful.

For many years the Stubbs and Taylor families told the story of how Butch Cassidy bought the Blue Creek ranch in the spring of 1890, next to the Bar C, and sold it again late that fall. The ranch still lies west of Barnum, where Blue Creek comes out of a canyon of its own.

There appears by that time to have been a loose organization of thieves moving horses great distances across the West. One route linked the Dakotas to Utah by way of the south Bighorns, Wind River and Jackson Hole—similar to the Astorians' route from 1811. Another route split south from the Bighorns across the Sweetwater, the Union Pacific and the Red Desert to Brown's Hole, where Wyoming, Utah and Colorado join. Either of these routes would have run right past the Blue Creek and Bar C ranches.

As the West filled up, it became necessary to sell the horses farther and farther from where they'd been stolen. This meant relays of wranglers, middlemen to move the money, and safe pastures en route. There could be no better country than the Red Valley for these purposes, with its good grass, isolation, and semi-cooperative neighbors.

Butch Cassidy was still using his real name, Bob Parker, when he and three associates robbed the San Miguel Valley Bank in Telluride, Colorado June 24, 1889. They escaped into southeastern Utah, but were too well known there to linger, and gradually moved north, with help from friends in Brown's Hole. Bob Parker, now known as George Parker or perhaps George Cassidy, began ranching in the fall of that year with his friend Al Hainer on Horse Creek, some miles above where it joins Wind River at present Dubois, Wyoming. Simpson family lore has Cassidy celebrating Christmas with them that year at Will Simpson's ranch on Wind River. (The lawyer Will Simpson was the father of Wyoming Governor and U.S. Senator Milward Simpson, grandfather of U.S. Sen. Al Simpson and his brother Pete.)

After the hard winter of 1889-90, Cassidy and Hainer cooperated with their neighbors on spring roundup, then sold their horses locally, closed up the ranch, and left without telling anyone.

Next, Butch turned up on Blue Creek, where he acquired 160 acres and before long, 420 more, and improved the place with outbuildings and irrigation ditches.[12] The Riverside post office, according to this version, was in Cassidy's original homestead cabin, fortified with rifle ports.

Jim Stubbs, who'd been cowboying around Barnum for three years or more, was at a Christmastime dance on the NH Ranch, Plunkett's old headquarters on Beaver Creek. At the dance Stubbs was approached by a boy, who told him there was a man outside who wanted to see him. Jim went outside, and made a deal on the spot with Cassidy, and forked over fifteen hundred dollars in gold for the ranch. Butch had to be leaving shortly, and promised to send the deed later. About a year later, Rap Harrell, supposedly a mixed-blood Sioux, showed up from South Dakota by way of the Bighorn Basin, and handed Stubbs a tobacco can, with the ranch deed folded up inside it.[13]

Great story; unfortunately, it's almost certainly not true. Jim Stubbs is listed as the earliest patentee on Blue Creek, in 1901, so there wouldn't have been a deed prior to that.[14]

Whether Cassidy was ever behind the Wall or not, however, some of his more criminal friends clearly were. Best known among these were Flat-nosed George Currie and the Logan brothers Johnny, Lonny, and Harvey, often known in Wyoming as the Roberts brothers, and in Montana (to confuse matters further) as the Curry brothers. The Logan brothers reportedly cowboyed on various Wyoming outfits and by the early nineties were operating regularly with Currie. They left Wyoming before the Invasion and drove a herd to Montana, where they homesteaded near the Little Rocky Mountains and what later became the town of Landusky. But after Harve Logan killed Pike Landusky in December 1894, he returned to the Red Wall country.

It may be no coincidence, then, that in October 1895, Wyoming newspapers began referring to a "Hole in the Wall gang," or "band," described as forty or fifty riders strong, well organized, stealing cattle routinely, and making clear the country was a place where deputies, stock detectives, and representatives of the big cattle outfits to the south and east were not welcome. Other papers disputed such reports as rumor and exaggeration.[15]

By the mid-nineties then, there was a law-enforcement vacuum in southern Johnson County. Failure to bring either the fifty-some invaders or the three killers of George Wellman to justice must have contributed to mixed feelings about the law. Everyone was trying to make a living, and most did not inquire too closely into their neighbors' ways.

Gradually, there came to be roughly three classes of people in the country. These included, first, outlaws—hardened criminals, usually without steady domiciles, who, when they weren't robbing banks or trains, stole livestock and moved it over long distances. The second category included ranchers who rustled on the side. These were mostly men with families in their present or future, who held property and could generally be found on their land. Many also did not mind increasing their small herds by now and then branding an unbranded animal. Third were genuinely honest ranchers.

George Currie and the Logans were in the first category. Currie, like Cassidy, had a genial reputation, but Harvey Logan was a killer. So too was Henry Smith.

In the second category were Nate Champion and men like Lou Webb, Tom Gardner, Al Allison, and Billy Hill, Jack Flagg's partners on the Hat Ranch, all of whom by 1891 were running cattle in the old Bar C pasture. Also in this category were the Smiths, Al and George, and their brother-in-law Bob, also named Smith. Al and George were sons of John R. Smith, a former freighter in the Indian Wars who stayed, and homesteaded on Crazy Woman Creek.

Best known to posterity among the honest ranchers is

Albert Brock, who acted as peacemaker at a crucial time. But even he understood it was in his interest not to ask too many questions.[16]

# Bob Divine
## and
## the Second Invasion of Johnson County

By the fall of 1896, Wyoming newspapers were reporting that big outfits were losing five hundred calves a year to thieves from the Hole in the Wall, and Natrona County Sheriff H. L. Patton was determined to do something about it.[17] The real push for action, however, came not from law enforcement but from the big ranches themselves.

All that year, the tough-minded, teetotaling Confederate veteran Bob Divine, foreman of the CY Ranchnear Casper, had been reporting constant trouble from George Currie and other thieves on tributaries of the Powder. Divine wrote regularly to his boss, Ed David, at the SO Ranchon Boxelder Creek between Glenrock and Douglas. David managed the SO and CY ranches for U.S. Senator (later Governor) Joseph Carey; the Careys also

Bob Divine, ex-Kansan, Confederate veteran,
and foreman of the CY Ranch, led two little-known invasions
of the Hole-in-the-Wall country in 1897.
Here he sits in front of his three sons, Tom, George, and Lee, in 1893;
Bob and Lee both survived the Hole in the Wall fight.
*Photo by G. H. Moore, David Collection,*
*Casper College Western History Center.*

owned the YU Ranchon the Greybull River in the Bighorn Basin. CY cattle ranged north from the Platte all the way to Powder River, sometimes turning up as far west as Lost Cabin or as far north as the Bar C Pasture, with worked-over brands.

"I am just of the same opinion as you," Divine wrote; "if any outfit in Wyoming is entitled to help catch those thieves it ought to be the CY." He feared Currie and fellow thief Tom O'Day were getting ready to leave the area and take with them a lot of "burnt cattle"—animals whose brands had been changed—to Montana or Nebraska for sale. The Carey interests had worked hard to get sheriffs Patton of Natrona County and Al Sproal of Johnson County elected. Both had promised to rid the country of thieves but results so far, Divine noted, were few.[18]

That spring, tensions continued to rise. In April, a Johnson County deputy named William Deane rode alone from Buffalo down to Powder River to arrest some rustlers.

He spent the night at Brocks', and next morning was confronted by two or three of the Logan brothers at the Griggs' post office on the Middle Fork. The Griggses managed to prevent any killing, but Deane continued on down the road toward Kaycee. When he came to the Kaltenbachs' corrals, he found Jess Potts overseeing a sheep-shearing operation and Mrs. Potts cooking for the crew. She invited the deputy in for lunch but he was rude to her, saying he needed no invitation to go where he pleased. At that point the Logan brothers and George Currie rode up. Deane ran shooting out of the house, and was killed by a rifleman from a nearby hilltop. The newspapers blamed the Logan brothers for the murder, though, as with the Wellman murder, the county didn't bring a case.

Elmer Brock, Albert's son, always insisted neither Currie nor the Logans killed Deane, but never would say who had done the crime.[19]

The following month, May 1897, the CY roundup began working all the country north and west of Casper. Divine's letters back to Ed David show a growing frustration, anger, and refusal to be intimidated. As the roundup moved through, rustlers routinely moved ahead of it, scattering the cattle and slowing the work, and then moving in behind the roundup to brand any cattle that had been missed. The day Divine moved north down Buffalo Creek through the Bar C pasture, he reported, four men followed him the whole time. Sheepmen had warned him the rustlers were preparing an ambush, and Divine's top hand Dan Sullivan had sent word of the same thing. Divine took the cattle by a different route, however—and avoided, this time, a confrontation.

And he named about a dozen names, including "Harve Ray" (Harvey Logan); Tom O'Day; George Currie; Al, Bob, and George Smith; Ed Starr (a George Wellman murderer); and "two Robberts who helped kill Dean"—that is, two other Logan brothers. He estimated there were twenty men altogether in the camp of his enemies.[20]

Everyone who knew Bob Divine in Natrona County seems to have remembered him as an honest, fearless man. But in Johnson County, people felt he was lumping some relatively honest rustlers in with hardened thieves.

At the same time, bad feeling had existed for some time between Divine and the Smiths. That spring, Al and George Smith decided it was time to leave the Hole in the Wall country, and sold their ranch at the mouth of Buffalo Creek canyon, at the south end of the Red Valley about ten miles upstream from the Bar C, to a sheepman. The buyer did not insist they leave immediately, and gave them time to round up their stock.

Divine may have known of the sale, and assumed the Smiths were rounding up stolen stock to drive out of the country. They were further delayed by the illness of Omie Smith, Bob Smith's wife and Al and George Smith's sister.

The Smiths' version of things was that they were simply waiting for the CY roundup, so they could look through the herd for stock of their own. Whose cattle were whose, who had a right to use which range—it was all the same questions that had led to Champion's feud with the Tisdales, six years before, and to many others in the country. Families like the Smiths, who saw the Hole in the Wall country as their own, might understandably have resented its being flooded with CY cattle every year. If the CY is going to take our grass, they reasoned, we might take a cow or two in return.

Then, on June 26, six men including George Currie, Harvey Logan, Harry Longabaugh (a.k.a. the Sundance Kid), and Tom O'Day, held up the Butte County Bank in Belle Fourche, South Dakota, near the Wyoming border. No one was hurt, but there was some miscellaneous shooting, the horses spooked, and the outlaws had to leave town in a hurry. O'Day's horse departed without him, and he was captured and jailed. The rest split up, heading for Lost Cabin and Thermopolis, Wyoming—destinations that almost certainly took them back to the Middle Fork, past the Bar C, and over the mountain. Press reports omitted that the bandits had collected at most a few hundred dollars. Still the newspapers followed the chase closely and reported various captures that never occurred. After a week or two, however, it was clear the posses were not going to catch the bandits, by now known in nearly all reports as the gang from that impenetrable hideout, the Hole in the Wall.[21]

By July, with the spring roundup completed, Bob Divine

had had enough. He and Ed David decided it was time to make a move in force. Divine, his son Lee, a CY cowboy named Tom McDonald, Ogallalla ranch foreman Bill Rogers and two of his cowboys, Pugsley ranch foreman Ike Dedman and two cowboys, a rep for the Half Circle L Ranch, and two stock detectives representing Montana cattle interests, Jim Drummond and the notorious Joe LeFors, headed together for the Hole in the Wall. The twelve men ostensibly meant to round up CY, Ogallalla, and Pugsley cattle.[22] But the main spring roundup was already past. Given the tension everywhere, and subsequent events, it seems more likely their main purpose was to force a fight. It was a second invasion of Johnson County.

According to Divine, the twelve men took their chuckwagons and cavvies with them through the Bar C Gap, and began working south up Buffalo Creek, rounding up CY cattle as they went. By the middle of the second afternoon, they'd had no trouble, they were near the top end of the valley, and were moving a herd of 170 animals. Here they met Al Smith, his brother-in-law Bob Smith, and their friend Bob Taylor, riding north. Of all the Smiths—perhaps of all the rustlers and thieves—Divine seems to have had his deepest grudge against Bob Smith, for reasons still not clear.

The parties, Divine later told the *Natrona County Tribune*, exchanged polite words, and began passing through each other, when suddenly Bob Smith wheeled his mount, called Bob Divine a son of a bitch, drew his pistol and shot. The bullet hit Bob Divine's horse in the neck and the horse fell. Bob Divine shot back and missed. Bob Smith shot again, the bullet slightly creasing Bob Divine's side. Bob Smith again turned his horse and fired a third time, again missing. Divine then took his own pistol in both hands, aimed carefully and fired, hitting Bob Smith in the back. The bullet went all the way through him and came out in front. He fell forward onto his horse's neck, rode another hundred yards or so, and fell.

In the dust, confusion, gunshots and pitching horses, Lee Divine was wounded in the fleshy part of his forearm, and Al Smith's gun was shot out of his hand. Several of the other cowboys galloped off when the shooting started. Bob Taylor surrendered, perhaps without firing at all. When the dust cleared, Bob Smith was on the ground, badly wounded and begging for water. When Bob Taylor started for the creek, to get water in his hat, Divine threatened to kill him; Taylor got the water anyway.

Not long afterward, three more friends of the Smiths rode up; the CY men disarmed them, but allowed them to help Bob Smith back toward what until recently had been the Smiths' cabin at the mouth of Buffalo Creek canyon, a mile and a half to the north. Their friend Tom Gardner then appeared, and helped also, but refused to be disarmed—saying he hadn't bought his pistol in order to give it away.

Omie Smith, still at the cabin and still not entirely recovered from her illness, had Gardner and the other friends load a mattress onto a buckboard to go retrieve her dying husband. He took all night to die, admitting he'd shot first. But he added that when they passed each other, he saw Divine already had gun in hand "down behind his leg. I thought I'd better get to shooting or I'd be dead." He urged his family not to try and avenge his death, and died around nine o'clock the next morning.

Taking Bob Taylor with them, the cattlemen released the cattle they'd rounded up and galloped back to the Bar C where they'd left their wagons, recovered them, and headed back for Casper. At the Bar C a woman warned them she expected more trouble, as a party of twenty armed men had recently passed by.

The Smiths' cabin near the mouth of Buffalo Creek Canyon, better known as the Hole in the Wall Cabin, shown here a year after Bob Smith died in it.
*Courtesy of Hoofprints of the Past Museum.*

Different versions of the fight begin to diverge even more drastically, however; Bob Taylor years later told his good friend Church Firnekas that the CY men had not come into the valley by way of the Bar C Gap, but by way of the Spring Creek Gap, directly west of Tisdales' and near the south end of the valley—there was no reason for them to detour so far north. They never took any wagons with them behind the wall, but left them, Taylor said, at Tisdales'. And the fact that the twelve men were riding together when they encountered him and the Smiths showed clearly, he said, that they weren't looking for cows; they were looking for trouble.

They exited the valley not by the Bar C Gap, but by the way they'd come in, out Spring Creek Gap, a much shorter route to Tisdales' and safety. They started telling Taylor what they were about to do to him, but he reminded them he had a lot more friends in that country than they did, and had, at that point, a chance a hundred times better of coming out alive. He regretted this threat years later, he said, as it made them hurry even faster away from Hole in the Wall.[23]

# A Third Invasion

Shortly after his return to Casper that summer of 1897 Divine received a letter threatening his life if he should come back north—"you must stay out or die you had better keep your d— outfit out if you want to keep them don't stick that d— old gray head of yours in this country again if you don't want it shot off." Divine turned the letter over to the *Natrona County Tribune*, and calmly began rounding up support for a second attempt. This time the force would be bigger than the original Johnson County Invasion, five years before. And it would include actual, legal, police. Along with the CY Ranch contingent this time came ten Natrona County deputies, fifteen Montana stock inspectors, Johnson County Sheriff Al Sproal, and Sheriff Butts from Belle Fourche, hoping for bank robbers. There were fifty-four men. On July 30, they approached from the south, by way of Willow Creek and the Spring Creek gap, and worked north down Buffalo Creek along the Red Wall.

They saw warning notices, but for two days had no trouble. On the third day, five men approached to a distance of about 125 yards, dismounted, and lay flat with rifles aimed at the invaders. Sproal rode up to them and said the little army had come peacefully, looking only for cattle, and the five rode away. Supposedly there were fifteen more men nearby, ready to back the play of the first five, but it didn't come to that.

The roundup moved on down Buffalo Creek, past the Bar C, down the Middle Fork and over to the North Fork, watched closely all along by the locals, including respectable ones like Tom Gardner and Lou Webb. By this time around five hundred head had been gathered. To simply drive these cattle out of the country would have amounted to a declaration of war; things at this point could have gotten bloody and no one, it seems, understood this better than Albert Brock.

Brock at that time was a state representative, ranching both sheep and cattle. People on all sides of the brimming feuds and resentments respected him. He had been in Pennsylvania at the time of the fight ten days earlier, and was now just back. On his own initiative he visited the cowmen's camp at suppertime, was invited to stay, dined, and explained why the locals were so angry. Could they ride in and inspect the herds for cows of their own? Divine and the rest agreed, and even offered to turn any disputed animals over to Sproal's custody, so that ownership could be legally established if necessary.

The work next day turned up only small problems. A calf with Alex Ghent's brand on it—Ghent was one of the Smiths' neighbors on Buffalo Creek—was following a Montana cow. The chief Montana detective sent word to Ghent to come get the calf; he didn't show. Johnny Nolen of the KC Ranch refused to claim another animal that had his brand on it, saying he didn't know quite how the brand had gotten on there. Lou Webb gave up a steer to the outfit that claimed it, saying he'd bought it in good faith. And that was it.

This third invasion of the Powder River country had recovered somewhere between four hundred and five hundred head for the different outfits, including eight Montana cattle. There is no way to tell how many of these were ordinary strays and how many had been stolen. Also found, however, were forty or fifty head with changed or burnt-over brands, and twenty-eight big steers on which the Ogallalla's keystone brand had been cut and skinned right off the living animals, and the edges sewn together afterwards. "This atrocity," notes the best historian of the event, "shocked even a local opinion...not generally sensitive to the feelings of animals." Years later, she notes, it emerged that George Currie had done the deed.[24]

As for Bob Taylor, he was jailed briefly in Casper, and then was moved to Buffalo after it was determined the gunfight had taken place in Johnson, not Natrona County. Before long, charges against him were dropped, and he was released.

But it's not as if peace came in any rush to the Red Wall country. That country stayed in the news; newspapers clearly liked the idea of outlaw hideouts by red-rock walls. At the same time cattle theft continued, and Bob Divine continued confronting it. In the fall, he and his top hands Dan Sullivan and John "Happy Jack" Allen left Casper on just two hours' notice that someone had rounded up eighty-three head of CY cattle in the south Bighorns, and was starting the bunch north. They caught up with the bunch on Crazy Woman creek, finally headed it off, and whoever was driving the cattle galloped off "spurring and whipping" in a great hurry. There proved to be twenty-one Ogallalla cattle mixed in; the group drove all back to Casper and shipped the Ogallalla cattle to their owners.

And the better-known thieves, meanwhile, remained in the district. "Only a week ago," the same news item continued, "it was currently reported that Harve Ray and Geo. Currie had gone to Alaska [the Klondike rush had just begun], but the news has come to Casper that they were both seen up in the vicinity of the Bar C Rancha few days ago. So it seems they are being harbored there and some fine night they will be swooped down upon and taken to prison just as their friends and companions have been before them."[25]

Still, the thieves remained successful for some time. In 1898, the nation went to war with Spain. According to bandit lore, there was a big gathering that spring of hard riders and quick shooters in Steamboat Springs, Colorado. They all nearly agreed to join up with Col. Torrey's rough riders, then preparing to invade Cuba. But the more they talked, the more they realized their enlistments might set them up for grand larceny arrests, and the idea vanished. Still, everyone present promised to hold off on crime until the war was over. By fall, the war was over. Some old acquaintances who'd freshened up their friendships at Steamboat agreed it was time to pull another job. Wyoming was still a pretty empty place—and a person on the run could always find friends, fresh horses and grub up around Hole in the Wall. How about a hit on the Union Pacific?

The Wild Bunch, 1900.
Left to right: Harry Longabaugh (the Sundance Kid), Will Carver,
Ben Kilpatrick, Harvey Logan, and Butch Cassidy.
Of these five in the famous photo taken in Fort Worth,
Longabaugh, Logan, and Cassidy robbed the Union Pacific at Wilcox,
and Longabaugh and Logan escaped through the Hole in the Wall country.[26]
*Courtesy American Heritage Center, University of Wyoming.*

# The Wilcox Robbery

About two hours after midnight on the morning of Friday, June 2, 1899, the U.P.'s westbound Overland Flyer was held up near the section house at Wilcox, Wyoming, ten miles east of Medicine Bow. A bandit on board persuaded the engineer to stop where he saw two red lanterns up ahead in the darkness. They had the trainmen uncouple the passenger coaches, and pull the train a short distance forward until it was on the far side of a bridge over a draw. Then they dynamited the bridge, to prevent a second train, expected soon, from coming closer.

When the clerk inside the express car proved less than cooperative, the outlaws set a charge under the doorsill and blew off the door. Inside they found a promising safe and an unconscious clerk. They dragged him to safety and tried more dynamite on the safe, blowing its door through the roof of the car, and scattering banknotes far into the rainy dark. Plenty of loot remained, however—cash, gold, jewelry, and perhaps as much as sixty thousand dollars, in unsigned banknotes. They packed the haul in their saddlebags, and rode off into the sagebrush. The first light of day was graying the sky.

Posses outfitted the next day and rode out in force from Laramie and Rawlins; guards were sent to Alcova on the North Platte to catch the bandits if they tried to cross there.

Though there was much confusion on the question at the time, outlaw scholars now seem to agree there were at least five bandits. Four rode north: Harvey Logan, who had been first to show his pistol to the engineer; George Currie; Harry Longabaugh; and a certain Billy Cruzan. Butch Cassidy had been there too, watching the whole time from the head of a draw some distance away. He escaped west and south.

Forty-eight hours after the holdup, the saloon was still open in Casper between one and two a.m. that Sunday morning when riders were spotted in the street. Someone joked that they were probably the train robbers, but no one really gave it much thought. The riders tried to rouse Charlie Bucknum at his livery stable for grain and a night's lodging for their horses. But he refused to do business in the middle of the night.

Next morning, on Casper Creek six miles north of town, a sheepherder out looking for his strayed horses came across a shack. It looked unoccupied; then he saw some horses, not his, and stopped to ask after his own. A man stepped through the door with two Winchesters, and handed one of them to a second man who followed him out. They hadn't seen any other horses, the first man said, and perhaps the herder should be moving on out of there. Which he did, quickly, right into Casper to report what he'd seen.

# Flight to Hole in the Wall

In Casper, a posse of about a dozen men was quickly assembled by Natrona County Sheriff Oscar Hiestand and Converse County Sheriff Joe Hazen, who must have hurried over from Douglas on a train. Lee Divine was in the group. Hurrying, undersupplied, they set out north for the sheepherder's shack to pick up the trail.

Probably late that Sunday afternoon, the bandits split up, with George Currie heading west for the Thirty-three Mile Trail, which would take him north to Buffalo Creek and the Red Wall country. The other three camped that night on Teapot Creek, still unchased as far as they knew. Next morning, Longabaugh stayed with the loot while Logan and Cruzan went out after their strayed horses. Shots rang out from some pine trees a few hundred yards off, and the two bandits knew they'd been discovered. They scrambled and ran, over a couple of low

divides to Castle Creek, south of present Midwest. Here, in
some rocks, they stopped and waited. It was now late morning
Monday, June 5. With his rifle, Logan shot at the first man
who appeared around a rock. The man went down, bleeding,
with a groan. Still on foot, Logan and Cruzan fled north, toward
Kaycee, thirty miles off, leaving Longabaugh to make his
own way with the loot. Logan and Cruzan had mortally
wounded Joe Hazen.

At Kaycee, the fugitives hid in brush until young Jobie
Gant came by. The young man remembered all his life how they
gave him battered-looking silver dollars and sent him into town
for food. Just as he was about done with the purchase, the posse
showed up. Young Jobie decided to let the robbers fend for
themselves. On they went, up the Middle Fork and up the Red
Fork to the Gardner Ranch, then over The Horn—the south end
of Gardner Mountain—back down, and then up to the top of
EK mountain, islanded out to the east of the main range. All this
was to throw off their pursuers.

News was out that the bandits had killed a sheriff, and the
Union Pacific was paying five dollars a day for deputies. Sixty
strong, nearly all of them deputized as sheriffs or U.S. marshals,
the posse assembled at Plunkett's old headquarters, the EK
Ranch. There they found sixteen year old Elmer Brock, looking
after a herd of saddle horses.

Word had filtered out the bandits were, in fact, on top of
EK mountain. The posse, still growing, surrounded it on all
sides and soon, one hundred nervous, armed men started up. But
the Brocks needed a herd of their horses that also was on top,
"so I went up and got them," Elmer remembered thirty-eight
years later. "The only precaution I took was to take my gun off
my saddle, as I knew the train robbers, or at least, their leader."
Took his gun off his saddle, that is, so he'd be unarmed and

wouldn't be mistaken for a deputy. The bandit he knew was the quiet, unassuming George Currie, who some years earlier had helped Elmer pack out the first deer he'd ever killed as a boy.

The posse surrounded the mountain and began a drive, moving up through the woods in a closing circle toward the top. They scared up nothing but an old grizzly sow. When they got to the top they found that the bandits, if they'd ever been there at all, had given them the slip.

Next morning, the posse was still at the EK, eating up all the Brock grub, when Alex Ghent came walking in. He said he was on his way with a load of salt to the Billy Hill ranch, but his team had played out. He'd hobbled them, but they'd gotten away the night before. The posse by now believed, correctly, that the bandits' escape had been on fresh horses from the Billy Hill ranch. There was old, bad feeling between Ghent and some of the deputies from Buffalo. (It was Ghent's brand the detectives had found on a calf following a Montana cow, two years before.) Before long several of the deputies started saying that now that the bandits had fresh horses, there was little chance of catching them: they might as well hang Ghent and call it a day.

Ghent understood what was up. He armed himself with a six-shooter and strode out into the midst of nearly one hundred armed men. He'd heard talk of a hanging, he said, and, cursing them fiercely, said they might carry it out but that there would be six who wouldn't enjoy it at all. They threatened to arrest him, but he refused to submit, as they had no warrant. And so, ironically, they deputized him. That way they could at least keep an eye on the old rustler and keep him under guard, without having to disarm him.

Some newspaper reports said the posse eventually totaled two hundred men. As the trail cooled, one English and two Cuban bloodhounds, a specially trained threesome, were brought on a special train to Casper from Beatrice, Nebraska, and sent north. No luck, of course. Wyoming Governor Richards authorized a five hundred dollar reward and the secretary of war authorized U.S. Marshal Hadsell to deputize as many men as he needed. But the bandits were among friends, or at least among a population that had other business than turning them in.

The bandits ended up, by some reports, in Lost Cabin, and later linked up with Cassidy at a saloon and hog ranch in East Thermopolis. They celebrated for several days and divided the loot. Then they rode off south toward Brown's Hole and the Utah canyon lands, then New Mexico, and into the memory of the West, and never were charged with the crime.[27]

But on Powder River, the Invasion of 1892, Bob Divine's intrusions five years later, and the escape of the train robbers two years after that were all part of a single chain of events. They involved many of the same people, much of the same country and travel routes. The Bar C, then, like the buffalo jump a thousand years before, was at a crossroads of everyone's route from somewhere to somewhere else. Laid over those routes in the 1890s was a network of grudge, feud, tension, and flight that wore away only very slowly, as the creeks and meadows became a little more settled, and unsettled scores drifted slowly into the past.

# Chapter 5
## Through the 20th Century

# A HISTORY

Famous ranches often become famous for staying in one family for a long time: the King Ranch in Texas is a good example, or the Sun Ranch on the Sweetwater River in Wyoming. In the Hole in the Wall country, the Taylor, Graves, and Brock-Hanson ranches on the forks and tributaries of Powder River are well known for similar reasons. But the Hole in the Wall Ranch—the former Bar C—is probably more typical, in that it's been held by a dozen or more owners since Peters and Alston abandoned it about 1890.

No detailed written accounts of the Bar C since that time have surfaced, with one important exception. Still, there are plenty of clues. In the early decades, owners Charles King and Alexander Cunningham were prominent in Wyoming business circles, and their land, banking, and business deals, along with their trips to the Bar C, were often noted in newspapers. The Burkes, who ran sheep on the Bar C in the 1930s and 1940s, are still well known, and are well remembered from that time by other Irish-American sheep-ranching families in central Wyoming. And finally, members of families that owned the Bar C since the Burkes still remember the ranch well, and were glad to talk about it.

The Wolds have had part or all of the ranch since 1980, and have now owned it much longer than anyone else. Like earlier owners, they keep it both as a business proposition and as a place to enjoy. Also like earlier owners, they do not live full time at the ranch, but depend on a manager and his family to run things day to day.

The single, detailed account of the ranch in its early days came from Elizabeth Lea Rawson, who in the late 1940s and 1950s wrote out her memories of her early life. Her family set out on a remarkable journey shortly before the turn of the last century. She was only a teenager, and she was known then as Lizzie Lea.

# On the Road

In the spring of 1898, the Leas sold their farm on the Missouri River in Boyd County, Nebraska and headed for Wyoming to buy wild horses. Anna Lea and her husband Frank had four children. Lizzie, sixteen, the oldest, was followed by Dick, Fannie, and Loyd, his name spelled with just one L. Loyd was two.

Frank Lea liked horses and clearly was good with them, and his children seem to have felt the same way. Lizzie, at least, loved to ride a good horse fast. Frank sometimes ran his horses in races, and gambled on them. He was a strong Populist, a lover of Shakespeare and English history, and could turn any number of skills toward earning a wage: he was a miner, sheep shearer, sheepherder, and cattle rancher as much as he was a gambler.

Within eighteen months the Leas would come to live and work on the Bar C ranch. But their harrowing life in the meantime is the kind of story often left out of history books. The depression of the 1890s had thrown thousands of families like the Leas off their farms and onto the roads. By Lizzie's account, the Leas seem to have lived primarily on sage chickens and hope.

It looked to be a good year for the horse business. The war with Spain had just begun, and the Army was buying horses. The Leas set out on their trip with four horses, a wagon, and a second wagon borrowed from an uncle. On the Fourth of July, they stopped at Chadron, Nebraska, and camped by the racetrack. Dick took their fastest horse, Billie, over to the track, to see if there was anything to be won in the Independence Day races. A new town like this, where the horse was unknown, often proved profitable. Years later, Lizzie couldn't remember if they won money. She remembered only sitting in the shade of the wagon with her mother, sister, and baby brother in the heat, waiting for Frank, Dick, and Billie the horse to return.

Soon, illness found them and took its toll. They were still in Nebraska when Anna miscarried, and hemorrhaged badly. Lizzie remembered blood all over the wagon bed. When they reached Glenrock, Wyoming, Anna was still very weak. One by one, the rest of the family came down with high fevers; Fannie was the sickest. Lizzie kept on hauling water and cooking as best she could. Finally, Anna swallowed her pride and borrowed money for a doctor. He diagnosed Fannie with an inflammation of the bowels, and prescribed medicine and hot packs. There was no way the Leas could afford these remedies, and so the doctor suggested a less expensive cure—to cover Fannie in cloths soaked in turpentine and lard. By the next day, Fannie was able to sit up,

Lizzie's uncle Tom came from Nebraska on the train with the money to buy the horse herd—borrowed money, Lizzie believed—and Frank and Tom closed the deal they'd worked out on a visit to Glenrock earlier in the year.

They bought the herd from George Devoe, brother of Hank Devoe who'd been foreman of the Bar C in the 1880s. George was "the largest man I ever saw... His brothers were not such big men and all but George were heavy drinkers," Lizzie recalled. The unbroken horses ranged in the mountains south of Glenrock. When Frank and Dick at last were well, Lizzie rode out with them. George's son, Bert Devoe, helped them gather the herd. They started driving the horses east 150 miles back to Alliance, Nebraska.

The herd didn't bring as much as they'd hoped, so the Leas returned to Glenrock and Frank took a job in the coal mines there. It was dangerous work; they rented two rooms from a family whose son and father had been killed in the mines earlier that year. Still, with Frank earning a steady paycheck, the Leas at last had enough to eat. Anna rented a sewing machine and took in sewing. Before long, Frank's rough temperament showed itself. He fought the abusive mine foreman one evening after work, off mine property, and whipped him. This seems to have won him respect, rather than losing him his job. But by spring, he was restless again.

He moved the family to Casper, where he'd heard there was work shearing sheep. But the work was only for men familiar with powered shearing machines. Down to his last fifty cents, Frank walked into downtown Casper and got himself a job on the Houck Ranch. Grubstaked, the family—four horses, two wagons, four kids, Frank, and Anna—headed north up the Thirty-three Mile Road, for Buffalo Creek.

# Into the Hole in the Wall Country

It was May 1899. The grass had just begun to green. On the second day, the Leas had their first sight of the Buffalo Creek Valley and the Red Wall. The red soil, the new green grass, pines on the distant mountain slopes, and "patches of gray sagebrush… if an artist was to put those colors on canvas, the world would say they were too vivid to be true," Lizzie wrote, years later.

Ed O. Houck ran a big sheep operation out of a headquarters at the head of Buffalo Creek Canyon— Fort Houck, it was called. The Casper paper reported he ran "approximately 15,665 sheep."[1] In the years since the drought and blizzards of the late 1880s, and the cattle wars of the early and mid 1890s, the ranges of the south Bighorns had gone largely to sheep. Sheep made more money, everyone believed; banks lent money on flocks, and sheep men were expanding their herds.

It was still lambing time when the Leas arrived in May. Sheep were scattered all up and down the valley. No one lambed in sheds then; the ewes and their lambs just did their best on the open range. The sheep grazed on the mountains in summer and "out in the badlands," as Lizzie put it, in winter. At Fort Houck they found a two-room house, with a family already living in it, a half-dugout, half-log storage room, a log bunkhouse, a barn, a tool shed, and a small corral. The Leas stayed in the bunkhouse, with their two wagons as extra bedrooms.

This was still outlaw country and outlaw times; it was the same summer the Wild Bunch robbed the Union Pacific at Wilcox. Lizzie never forgot the evening the notorious horse thief Tom O'Day, (one of the Belle Fourche bank robbers two years earlier), rode in and joined the men at the supper table. The Leas were informed O'Day would get the bunkhouse. Young Dick, angry, left the bunkhouse but took the bedding with him. O'Day, uncomplaining, rolled up under his own saddle blanket, and left next morning before anyone was up.

The nearest neighbor to the Houck headquarters was a Mrs. Richardson, at a Houck cabin ten miles downstream near the mouth of Buffalo Creek Canyon.[2] But the Leas were sent to run a new haying operation ten miles further up the creek from Fort Houck. Frank and the family were to dig a ditch to water a hay meadow. They lived in tents, and plowed and planted a garden on the south side of the creek. It was hard work and outdoor living, and the children had little in the way of decent shoes or clothing. But at least Frank was around all the time, Lizzie remembered, and had nowhere to spend his paycheck.

Restless again, Frank decided after a month or two that the family needed a trip deeper into the mountains. Traveling north along the mountain crest, they came after two days to the headwaters of the Red Fork of Powder River and a place later called Cheeversville, or Cheever's Flats. Here there were shearing pens, people, and lots of activity.

Cooking for all comers was May Devoe, the same woman who had made the Bar C an oasis of sociability in the 1880s. The Devoes lived in one tent, and cooked meals in another, larger one. Lizzie remembered May as jolly and uncomplaining but Hank, the former Bar C foreman, was a "whiskey soak." May "cooked for the shearers and [Hank] drank up the money she made," Lizzie remembered. One day, when the women had left Loyd in a tent for a nap, a staggering Hank, hunting up a whiskey bottle, fell nearly on top of the child.

In a third tent another family, a mother and a teenage daughter, took in washing, and probably entertained the shearers in more personal ways. Ten years later, when Lizzie was in Casper for her father's funeral, she learned that the two of them were living "down on the Sandbar," the red-light district, "in a little shack and entertained any man who had a dollar."

Returning, the Leas traveled down Beaver Creek, past Barnum to the Bar C—never dreaming the ranch would soon become their home—then south up Buffalo Creek and back to the Houck headquarters at the head of the canyon for a new assignment. This time they were sent to the Hodge place, another one-roomed cabin and hay camp. Again, they were living in a tent and working hard. Lizzie remembered snakes, flies, and little food. The children gathered wild fruit, and frogs for their edible legs.

Though even food was scarce, Anna that summer found a way to order Lizzie "a lady's astride saddle" from the Montgomery Ward catalog. Old proprieties were changing.

Within a year, all women would be riding the same saddle as men, Lizzie remembered, but she was eager to be at the head of the fashion. To ride with her new saddle, her mother made Lizzie a pair of very full gray flannel bloomers.

The children got little schooling. That summer, Anna made no attempts to come up with lessons for them. But it may have been that Frank's love of history rubbed off on Lizzie. Between cutting hay and gathering wild food, she found time to memorize large chunks of *Barnes' Popular History of the United States of America*. A few years later, when she took the exam to become a teacher herself, the earlier study stuck with her. "Every history exam," she remembered, "called for the reasons for the Revolutionary War and I had them pat."

That fall, a man came to call one day when Frank was in the hayfield. He was Jack Rooney, new foreman of the Bar C Ranch. Charles H. King, a man with banking, mercantile, and real-estate interests in Casper and around the West had recently bought the ranch, rundown by then, and was looking to change it over to sheep. Rooney had heard Frank Lea was a good worker. He needed a man with a family—the man to work the place, the woman to cook for shearers and camp movers and any other crews that might come through. And so the Leas moved down Buffalo Creek to where it joined the Middle Fork of Powder River, and came to live and work on the Bar C Ranch.

# Life on the Bar C

The squared-log house Peters and Alston built in the 1880s had seen some hard use by this time, but it was still there, with its low porch and single story, eight rooms and seven fireplaces. By this time, the house was divided in half by a wall with no door in it. The Rooneys used half the living space; the Leas used the other half. Other rooms in back were kept as a bunkhouse and storerooms. The floors were pine and the roof, dirt.

House and outbuildings lay close to the river, and the children carried water from a little springhouse just west of the house. A short way north of the river was a smaller creek—Spring Creek—full of trout, with watercress along its edges in summer. "Imagine," Lizzie wrote, years later, "fresh fish and salad greens after the way we had been living."

There were miles of fence to be torn down and rebuilt, a

flock of bucks (rams), to be herded near the ranch, sheds to fix, hay to put up, and a hay meadow to care for. The Leas were welcome to keep milk cows, make cheese, and have a garden.

Anna cooked daily for her own family, the Rooneys—Jack, his wife, and their son—an English camp mover named Jack Perry, one or two hired men, and any company that might stop by—at least ten or twelve people at every meal. Cowboys in the country soon learned there was a pretty young girl at the Bar C—Lizzie—and company picked up. In spring, Anna cooked for the shearing crews, too. All her life Lizzie would remember the thick, strong sheep smell around the dinner table.

Fencing was the hardest job, but Frank figured out a way to speed it up. He had contracted for the work at so much per rod of fence line. Rooney had assumed Frank would do the work by hand, tearing the wire off the posts, and then pulling the posts out of the ground. But Frank used the wagon. He'd loosen the fence wire and attach it to the rear of the wagon bed. Then he'd have one child drive the wagon, slowly and steadily down the fence line, pulling the wire off the posts as it went. The posts must have been rotten or the staples rusty for this to work, but it did work. Then Frank would use the wagon again, attaching a chain to the posts and pulling them out "almost as fast as he could walk from one to the next," Lizzie remembered.

So while two Leas were working the fence line—perhaps Fannie driving the team and Frank working the posts and wire—Lizzie might have been out with the rams while Dick did general repairs. So much work got done so quickly that Rooney admitted to Frank he was nervous about submitting the bill. Frank replied, "Just tell him it isn't one man, but the whole damn family."

The Leas were also great cheese makers. Back in Nebraska, selling the cheese they'd made was often their only

The Leas and many others gathered at the Condit place near Barnum, about 1900.
Left to right: Anna, Fannie, Lizzie and Loyd Lea; Bill Stubbs; Hattie Backus; Mrs. Van Winkle; Mrs. Backus; Al Smith, who was at the Hole in the Wall fight; Earl Devoe, Mrs. Rooney; a man named Slim, Herman Rooney holding his mother's hand; and Dick Lea.
*Photo courtesy of Merle Kimball, from her book* Looking for the End of the Rainbow.

way to raise a little cash. In 1900, their first spring on the Bar C, they gathered a few cows off the range, began milking them, and making cheese in quantity. Frank hollowed a niche in the chimney where they set the cheese vat.

The Leas quickly got to know the other families along the Red Wall. The Keiths had the next ranch east, downstream on the Middle Fork. The Stubbses, their relatives the Backuses and later their relatives the Taylors had the next ranch north, on Blue Creek. (Mrs. Richardson, whom the Leas had first met on Buffalo Creek, was born a Stubbs). The Barnum family was on Beaver Creek where it bends east toward the Middle Fork— where their namesake "town" is now. Lizzie had swift, strong opinions about all these people—the Keiths were book readers and good friends, the Barnums were dirty and their children shoeless and wild; the Backuses were ignorant Texas trash, yet "very decent in every way," and so on.

Social life was lively. There were dances every second or third Saturday night behind the Red Wall. Once young Bert Devoe turned up, who had helped them trail the horse herd to Nebraska. He was very interested in Lizzie, and while the two of them were enjoying the pre-dance supper, Bert's uncle Hank came to their table, "too drunk to stand steady," she remembered years later. Hank talked for a while about the "Old Home Ranch." He may have meant the Bar C, but he was so drunk Lizzie and Bert couldn't tell; then he rambled on about the killing of Nate Champion and Nick Ray.

Entire families came to the dances; there was no babysitting and so the children were left to sleep while the adults danced all night. Women brought coffee and big baskets of food. There was little drinking; Lizzie never remembered dancing with a man who had liquor on his breath. Or if there was to be drinking, word went around ahead of time

The Barnum post office, 1914.
*Courtesy of the Johnson County Jim Gatchell Museum.*

and people who disapproved simply didn't go. People dressed up. Cowboys wore their best shoes; they never danced in their boots. That would have been like showing up in work clothes. And they never let out whoops and yells on the dance floor—that would have been rude.

Lizzie loved the short ride over to the post office at the Barnums' ranch, to get the mail. She had many correspondents and always rode hoping for news of the world. This was a sophisticated dissatisfaction for that time and place: "Though we had things nicer at the Bar C than any time since we went west, I was not happy with our surroundings," she remembered, years later. "I longed for the really better things of life, books, music, good clothes, companions of a higher standard than those around me." Yet she wished she were as content in her life as the Barnums were in theirs.

The Leas returned to Casper for the fall and winter of 1900-1901. Frank bought a house downtown and did odd jobs. Lizzie went to school for a few months. They were back on the Bar C the following spring and summer, back in Casper another winter, and in the spring of 1902, back on the Bar C. That fall, Frank landed the contract to haul mail from Wolton, near present Arminto west of Casper, by way of Barnum to Kaycee; he traveled the route several times per week. That winter, the Leas managed a hotel in Kaycee, while Lizzie visited her aunt in Iowa. She returned, and in the fall of 1903 got her first teaching job, at a country school farther down Powder River from Kaycee. The Leas then took over Jack Parry's homestead, just north of the Bar C, under Castle Rock. In the fall of 1904, Lizzie finally left the Red Wall country for good, taking a job at the Luman school near Hyattville on the west side of the Bighorns. There she met her future husband, Edward Rawson, who had the grocery store.

She seems to have been glad to put ranching behind her, though her life was by no means easy from then on.

Other Leas stayed behind the Red Wall on the homestead under Castle Rock at least until 1919. Lizzie's younger sister Fannie married Frank Graves in 1915, and they ranched on the old Dull Knife battlefield, where the north and south prongs of Red Fork come together. Graveses still ranch there today—all of them Lea descendants as much as they are Graves descendants.[3]

# Charles H. King

Like any ranch, the Bar C at the turn of the last century was a business as well as a family venture, and as a business it drew some of Wyoming's most interesting investors. They, too, brought their families to the ranch, occasionally to live, more often to visit.

T. W. Peters, one of the founders, did not file actual land claims on the Bar C until several years after he'd first brought in cattle. By the time he finally proved up, in 1892—when he first won clear patents in his and his wife, Minerva's names—he and Minerva had already sold their house in Cheyenne and probably had gone back to Philadelphia. In 1894, Frank Kemp, who had been Moreton Frewen's bookkeeper and manager in Cheyenne, bought Peters' land on the Middle Fork and Buffalo Creek. Kemp sold his interests to a Conrad Young two years later. In December 1897, Young sold his pieces to Charles H. King.[4]

King had been born in Pennsylvania in 1853. He is best known to history as the paternal grandfather of President Gerald R. Ford. But he seems to be the same Charles H. King who, with six others, was indicted on federal charges in 1886 in connection with a plan to swindle the government out of redwood-timber lands in California, and sell them off to Scottish investors.[5]

In the mid-1880s, King began investing in retail, freight, and banking businesses along the westward-building Fremont, Elkhorn, and Missouri Valley Railroad. He helped found Chadron, Nebraska, in 1884; Douglas, Wyoming in 1886; and Casper in 1888. King and his wife, Martha, started a family in Chadron. The family came with him to Wyoming.

He opened Casper's second bank, C.H. King and Company, in 1889, probably running it out of the dry goods store he owned at the same time. Both firms were small. His head clerk was Alexander J. Cunningham. Soon another partner joined them, DeForest Richards, who later would become governor of Wyoming. Richards owned a ranch on Canyon Creek, on the west side of the Bighorns; it may be through him that King began to think about expanding into the ranching business.

In April 1895, Wyoming papers reported that the Bar C had been leased by a syndicate of Boston wool merchants planning to run thirty thousand sheep, and that a local pioneer had leased Horace Plunkett's old NH Ranch with plans to run eighteen thousand more. The country on the headwaters of the Middle Fork was starting to look like "one vast sheep pasture, to the great disgust of the small cattlemen" in the district, the *Cheyenne Daily Sun* reported.[6] Yet those small cattlemen were still active; it would be two more years before Bob Divine and his posse rode north to Hole in the Wall.

In 1896, King sold his bank to Cunningham and Richards but kept the dry goods store. In 1897, he went into the cattle business with George Rhoades, who had a ranch south of Casper. They planned for Rhoades to live on the Bar C and run it, stocking it with his own cattle and adding to it with cattle purchases most likely financed by King.

Late in 1897, King bought the Bar C for a reported six thousand dollars. The ranch included about a thousand deeded acres, good ditches, a productive hay meadow, sheds, a barn, a big house, and good grazing on public land stretching in all directions.[7]

But while Rhoades remained a cattleman, King reversed himself and decided on sheep. The two parted ways.[8] It was part of a trend. While sheep numbers were exploding in Wyoming at the time, cattle numbers were declining.

Like so many others in those years, the Richards and Cunningham bank primarily financed sheep; probably it financed King's purchase of the Bar C and the flocks he stocked it with. And King, Richards and Cunningham all had close business ties to Omaha, where wool was shipped and stored and lambs were slaughtered.

Sheepmen generally borrowed money in the fall, with the winter flock as collateral. Loans would be renewed in early spring, with more money for operating expenses. After shearing, when the wool crop was sold in the late spring, these loans were partly paid off, with final settlement after fall lamb sales. The bank would bundle the loans and sell them to Richards' bank in Douglas, which bundled more loans and sold them again to the Omaha National Bank, all with the sheepmen's notes as security.[9] Sheep were a logical extension of all King's other businesses. They were a way to turn land into money.

In early September 1898 a reporter for Casper's *Wyoming*

Charles H. King and his family, about 1901.
Most likely these are, left to right: C.H. King, Martha Porter King, Leslie Lynch King, Savilla King, Charles B. King, and Marietta King. *Anderson collection, Casper College Western History Center photo.*

*Derrick* made a trip north. He traveled past the Tisdale ranch, then followed Wister and Bob Tisdale's route from seven years earlier, up Murphy Creek, through the Bar C Gap and down to the "the famous Bar C Ranch." Up the slope to the west, the reporter found a number of sheepmen at dipping pens or out with their flocks, including Houck, C.H. Townsend, Casper Mayor (and future U.S. Senator) Patrick Sullivan, and others. "It is understood," the paper reported, "there were at least 400,000 head of sheep on the Big Horn Mountains this year."[10]

That year King formed the Bar C Sheep Company, and the next spring brought in the flocks. Bar C foreman Jack Rooney was working for King by June 1899. Late that summer Rooney hired Frank Lea away from the Houck ranch. In the fall, King bought twenty railroad cars full of sheep—fifty-two hundred head—and had them trailed out to the Bar C. By then it was primarily a sheep operation. And so, largely, it would remain for fifty years.[11]

The Kings were also the first owners in more than a decade to use the ranch steadily as a place to bring guests; soon the Bar C was part of society news, too. Casper papers reported the Kings' sojourns to the Bar C for weekends or weeks, with guests and with their own children, Leslie, Savilla, Charles B., and Marietta.

But ranching does not seem to have held King's full-time interest for very long, if it ever did. When he sold a trainload of sheep in June 1902, he announced the Bar C was for sale, 1480 deeded and irrigated acres "with or without cattle." Perhaps he felt ranching was distracting him from what he was really good at—developing businesses in towns like Casper, Shoshoni, and Riverton, as the railroad arrived.[12]

About this time King took on Dan Sullivan as a partner on the Bar C, almost certainly the same Sullivan who had accompanied Bob Divine on trips to round up CY cattle. Sullivan and his wife threw a big Fourth of July picnic on the ranch in 1906, with songs, footraces, poetry recitations, music by the Beaver Creek orchestra, and a baseball game between the married and the single men. (The married men won.) All the familiar local families were there—Leas, Barnums, Devoes, Graveses, Carrs, and Frakers—and good-natured May Devoe ran the lemonade stand.[13]

The Kings moved to Omaha in the fall of 1905, and their daughter, Savilla, was married there the following winter.[14] King built a complex of wool warehouses in Omaha, but remained active in Wyoming. He invested in the Jackson townsite, and in 1908 became a director of a bank in Riverton, with his old Casper partner A.J. Cunningham as president.[15]

Late in 1907, King and Sullivan sold the Bar C to James Roush, who had some innovative ideas that didn't work out. Roush built a large lambing shed so that his ewes, protected from the weather, could lamb earlier in the year. But hay and grain were scarce that early in the spring, the ewes were undernourished and lacked sufficient milk, and the lambs died. Roush also built a new ditch that skirted the slopes of some hills—too closely, apparently, as the ditch wouldn't hold water and washed away down the slope.[16]

# Alexander J. Cunningham

King's former clerk, Alex Cunningham, meanwhile, was expanding into the sheep business, as King had before him. He ran a big shearing operation at Wolton in 1903. By the spring of 1907, his spring wool clip was the third largest in central Wyoming, at 200,000 pounds. Cunningham had a taste for the good life, vacationed at the gambling and horse-racing hub of Hot Springs, Arkansas, and built what is still one of Casper's finest houses, on the southwest corner of 11th and Center.[17] In 1911, a Cody newspaper reported Cunningham's plan to carry fifty-five thousand head of sheep through the coming winter, out of four million sheep expected to be wintered over that year in all of Wyoming.

Around that time, Cunningham bought the Bar C and brought in Dan Rhoades, probably a relative of King's former partner George Rhoades, to run it. They appear to have run cattle and sheep; in 1916, the Bar C was listed as the starting point for one of the last big cattle roundups on Powder River.[18]

Also like the Kings, the Cunninghams used the Bar C to entertain. In 1920 and 1921, Alex and Ada Cunningham went with Governor and Mrs. Robert Carey and an Irish banker, Sir Thomas Esmonde, on a hunting trip to Jackson Hole. Ada shot an elk the first season; the second she shot a moose, the head of which, the *Casper Daily Tribune* reported, would shortly hang on the wall in a new cabin at the Bar C. The following year Esmonde returned a third time, and visited the Cunninghams in Casper and at what the *Casper Herald* called "the Cunningham country home, the Bar C ranch."[19]

Cunningham remained a prominent banker. After World War I, agricultural prices plunged, and Wyoming was hit by severe drought and the worst winter since 1887. Farmers, ranchers, and their bankers were hit hard. In 1921 Cunningham worked to get federally backed credit flowing to Wyoming farmers and ranchers. By the end of 1921, $1.6 million in federally backed loans had been approved for the state out of four million dollars applied for. [20]

At the same time, people continued to take up free government land. Open range on the south end of the Bighorns was pretty much gone by the 1920s. By the end of the decade, most land south of the National Forest boundary was deeded. A 1916 change in the homestead law—a person could now file on an entire section at a time, instead of just a quarter section— had made this easier. Still, it remained up to landowners to fence out any unwanted stock, and few bothered. This allowed the bigger outfits to keep running their sheep pretty much where they always had, according to custom, water, topography—and now, roads.

Cunningham built a set of sheep corrals where the

Hazelton Road along the crest of the mountain crosses the Middle Fork of Powder River. The corrals were on the south side of the river and a little downstream from the crossing. Other sheep men also used these corrals, along with a second set, the Bar C corrals, farther south.

Cunningham built a store there on the Middle Fork, and another where the road crossed Buffalo Creek. These sold tack, hardware, dry goods, and beer, the last of which made them popular with the herders but not the flock owners. Most useful, the stores sold salt blocks for the livestock, which were heavy and difficult to ship in. The salt kept the stores in business for decades, until trucks got heavier and it was easier for sheepmen to haul their own.

But all of Cunningham's stores, sheep, and banks weren't enough to protect him from the agricultural slump that lasted straight on through the decade. He had invested heavily in irrigated land around Riverton, which fell in value, and his banks made too many loans to his ranching friends. He also appears to have borrowed against the Bar C from his own bank, now called the Casper National Bank. Late in 1930, he lost the ranch to the bank.

A year later, a smart, thrifty Irishman snapped it up.

# The Burkes

Mickey Burke came to Wyoming from County Cork in 1901, and went to work herding sheep for his cousin Patrick Sullivan, the former Casper mayor. He learned the business fast, was promoted to foreman, and by 1906 had saved enough to homestead north of Casper and start his own outfit, the Burke sheep company. His brother Patrick came out from Cork to join him. In 1914 Mickey married Anna McKenna, and they had five children: Frank, Joe, John, Kathleen, and Bill.

Mickey ran the sheep operations from town, though at the busy times of lambing, shearing, and shipping he was out with the sheep and the men; in late spring the entire family came out to the mountains. He always had an eye out for land when it came up for sale, or when homestead claims were relinquished by discouraged claimants. In 1924, he joined Peter and Nora Buckley to form the Cottonwood Sheep Company.

Already by then, Irish-American sheep operations were a tradition in the southern Bighorns. Most traced their roots and their relatives to John Mahoney, who came to America in 1870, got a job in a New Jersey boiler factory, and sent for his cousin Tim. When the jobs disappeared in a depression, they joined the Army and ended up at Fort Steele, east of Rawlins, Wyoming. After their discharge, Tim went to Denver and started stores; John went into the sheep business. Tim became Denver Tim; John became Rawlins John. John was the first to trail sheep into the Buffalo Creek drainage in the 1890s; supposedly he'd first seen the country while chasing deserters out of Fort Steele.

Key to the Mahoney holdings in the south Bighorns were two sections of state school lands on two forks of Buffalo Creek. But John Mahoney's son Phil, unfortunately a drinker who needed extra money, re-leased the sections for a premium. He failed, however, to split the extra revenue with the state, as the law required. Someone told on him, and he lost the leases. Mickey Burke picked them up, and eventually forced the Mahoneys to sell all their operations in the area, in June, when everything is at its lowest value—calves and lambs are small, and sheep recently shorn.

Late in 1931, Burke and Buckley's Cottonwood Sheep Company bought the Bar C Ranch. Hard times came to them too, however. Mickey and Anna's daughter Kathleen died of diphtheria when she was three. Mickey's brother, Patrick, routinely drank too much and was killed in a car wreck in 1929, while Anna died of tuberculosis not long afterward. Mickey subsequently married the former Della McKenna, Anna's sister and Patrick's widow. "She raised both families, bless her," another longtime Irish-American sheep rancher remembered years later.[21]

A favorite summer spot of the Burkes was near Cheever's

Joe Burke, no date.
The Burkes headquartered their sheep operations
in the southern Bighorns at the Bar C Ranch from 1931 to 1948.
*Casper Star-Tribune Collection,*
*Casper College Western History Center photo.*

Flats, the same Cheeversville the Leas had visited in 1899. In the mid-1930s it still had shearing pens, and a tent-town hotel, bar, and brothel. It was popular as ever with the herders and shearers, and unpopular with the men who owned the sheep. Later in the decade, Peter Buckley or Mickey Burke, or perhaps both, burned it down, "as it was a hazard to the safety of anyone who went there," one of the Graveses from the Red Fork remembered, years later.

In the thirties and forties the Burkes ran four summer bands of sheep, which took a lot of herders and camp movers year round. These would be flocks of about twelve hundred ewes, with their lambs. A sixty or sixty-five percent survival rate among lambs was considered good then. Soon the Burkes, like other outfits, began building lambing sheds, and the lambs' survival improved. In the fall the men would trail the sheep to the railroad at Arminto or Waltman to ship the lambs and old ewes. Then the Burkes would graze the sheep a few months on their land near the railroad, and only after Christmas would they trail them back to the good winter range on the mountain slopes above the Bar C.

As World War II approached, Mickey was determined to bring his sons full time into the ranching operations. Sheep ranching was considered vital to the war effort, and men engaged in it got draft deferments. Peter Buckley had been managing the Bar C, but now the Burkes bought him out. Buckleys bought the remains of the old NH Ranchnorth of Barnum on Beaver Creek, and moved there. Mickey's son, Joe Burke, took over management of the Bar C in 1942.

Finally in 1948, the Burkes broke up the Bar C and sold most of the pieces. They kept the land on the mountain slopes, but sold off tracts on Murphy Creek east of the Red Wall and stretching all the way to where the Interstate is now. Likewise

they sold the old ranch core at the Middle Fork-Buffalo Creek
confluence, which retained the name Bar C. The Burkes bought
the former Richards ranch in the Freezeout Range on the edge
of Shirley Basin, north of Medicine Bow, just in time for the
great Blizzard of 1949.[22]

# The Cronins

Two brothers from another Irish-Wyoming ranch family, Joe and Bernard (Barney) Cronin, bought the Bar C from the Burkes. Their father, Bill Cronin, had come to Wyoming before 1900, and later took on Con O'Connor as a partner. Like the Burkes, the Cronins ran sheep in the southern Bighorns. Bill Cronin had died in the mid-1940s.

Barney Cronin was a civil engineer and most likely financed the deal, but he "was pretty much hands off on the Bar C," his son Vaughn remembers now. Barney liked the fishing, but let Joe run the ranch. He was thrifty about it, keeping an old Model T truck running pretty well. The two brothers were close. They owned the ranch for eleven months.[23]

# The Baxters

In the spring of 1949, Sam and Hazel Baxter bought the Bar C from the Cronin brothers. The Baxters had moved to Casper from Oklahoma in 1938, and owned the Ada Apartments and Indian Ice in Casper. A news report of the sale gave the ranch's size by then at 5,080 deeded and six thousand leased acres, along with an 1885 water right. Baxters, the paper said, loved to hunt and fish, and thought the ranch's "blood red bluffs" would make a fine setting for a Technicolor western movie. The Baxters planned to restock the ranch with cattle.[24]

# The Hartnetts

In April 1951, Fred Hartnett of Casper and his partner Bill Deacon bought the Bar C from the Baxters. Hartnett was a hardworking refurbisher of oil tanks. He and his employees sandblasted, treated, and painted the tanks. It was loud, dirty, dangerous work, but he made good money at it. When he found his hearing getting worse, however, he left the tank business and began investing widely in uranium, oil, and real estate—including ranches.

He owned at least three besides the Bar C, one near Douglas, one near Pathfinder Reservoir, and one near Enterprise, Oregon. At other times he owned uranium claims near Moab, Utah, an oil well in Kentucky, real estate in San Francisco, and a bowling alley in Colorado. And he was the last owner of Casper's famed Henning Hotel, when it was torn down in 1973.

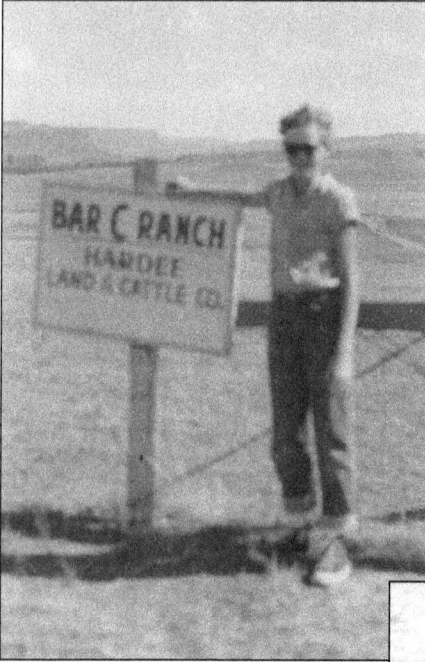

Hartnett cousin Dick Doty
at the Bar C, 1950s.
*Courtesy of
Connie Hartnett Henry.*

Connie Hartnett, with a snake in
her arms, on the Bar C about 1952.
*Courtesy of Connie Hartnett Henry.*

"Dad was always carrying a Geiger counter around at the ranch," his oldest daughter, Judy, remembers now. Fred's wife Hazel was only five feet tall and generally regarded as the brains of the outfit, her daughters say; when she stamped her size-four left foot, everyone paid attention. There were three daughters: Judy Hartnett Middleton, of Auburn, Washington; Constance (Connie) Hartnett Henry, who lives outside Casper; and Donna Hartnett Morgan, who died in the early1990s.

Connie and Judy remember summers at the Bar C when they were girls. Sometimes their parents would drive them up from Casper, a trip that seemed to stretch forever. Sometimes Fred would fly them up in his Piper Cub, or later a Super Cub, land in a pasture, and wheel the plane into a fenced enclosure

Left to right, Curt Simpson, Bill Deacon and Fred Hartnett
in Jackson Hole, about 1960.
*Courtesy of Connie Hartnett Henry.*

where the cows couldn't rub up against it.

From time to time a few close friends would visit to fish the Middle Fork, and once Fred invited the Sons of the Pioneers, who'd performed at the Natrona County Fair that summer, up to the ranch to fish. But generally, the girls remember their father as a person who seldom relaxed.

With Bill Deacon, Fred formed the Hardee (that is, Hartnett-Deacon) Land and Cattle Company. As manager they hired Rocky Thorpe. Still, Fred took an active part at branding, haying, and gathering the cows off the mountain before shipping in the fall. Hazel and the girls did, too, but Fred's greatest pleasure was the work.

The two sisters, meanwhile, had horses to ride, and the river was full of fish. Weekly trips to Kaycee for groceries and ice cream, and Saturday night dances at the Barnum Hall were adventures. Local ranches all helped each other at branding times. The girls were not allowed to climb Steamboat rock— wildcats up there, their parents told them—but otherwise seem to have been left largely to themselves. Connie has a memory from when she may have been as young as three, of being carried piggyback across the Middle Fork by her big sister Donna. Out of the blue Connie began singing *Waltz Me Around Again, Willie*, and Donna, surprised, laughed so hard that Connie got dropped in the water. Judy remembers being bucked off the albino foal of a palomino mare that their friends Curt and Babe Simpson boarded at the Bar C. "I hopped on, he took a few crow hops, and I ended up head first in the most oily gunk you ever saw," Judy said.

Both have memories of the big, cool barn. The barn and corrals were on the west side of the road. (A small log bunkhouse—the only building left from the ranch's earliest years—remains on the east side of the road.) The barn had stalls for the horses, a tack room, and hay in the loft, from where it could be dropped down to the horses. In a shop attached to the barn was a big grindstone for sharpening blades. The girls would pedal it, to make it turn.

In 1957, Fred sold the ranch—roughly nine thousand acres then, deeded and leased—for eighty thousand dollars. "It makes me cry every time I think about it," Connie says.[25]

# The Culvers

The oil business boomed in Wyoming in the mid-1950s. George Culver, an oilman from Newcastle, Wyoming, was flying a friend from Casper to Billings when he first saw the Hole in the Wall country from the air. Not long afterwards, Culver learned the Bar C was for sale, looked up Fred Hartnett, and they made a deal. Final papers still hadn't been signed, however, when Culver's plane crashed, killing him one snowy night as he flew from Billings back to Casper. Culver's widow, Elizabeth Lucille Culver, was not eager to own the Bar C after that, but Hartnett wouldn't let the family out of the deal, and so she went ahead with it.

The Culvers' son, Jerry, was allowed a hardship discharge from the Air Force to help his mother run the Bar C and another ranch near Upton. There was plenty of work, running Angus cattle and cutting alfalfa. Jerry didn't know much about ranching at first, his widow, Bonnie Culver, remembers now. But like his father and Fred Hartnett before them, Jerry kept tabs on his ranches by air. He hired a friend as foreman of the Upton ranch, and another friend, Dee Ray, as foreman at the Bar C.

Jerry's mother quickly tired of pumping money into the operation—for bulls and everything else, and in the spring of 1959 she leased the ranch to Jack Greer, of Gillette. Meanwhile the Culvers had known that Ernie Vest and his wife, Nola, of Casper, had wanted to buy the Bar C for years; Jerry approached them and they worked out a deal. The Vests agreed that if they ever decided to sell, they'd give Culvers a right of first refusal.[26]

# The Vests

Ernie and Nola Vest bought the Bar C from the Culvers in 1961. Jack Greer's lease ran five years, however, so it was 1964 before the Vests took over.

Ernie was an old hand at ranching. Born in Illinois, he served in France and Belgium in World War I, and came to Wyoming afterward to work for the famed cattleman H.W. "Hard Winter" Davis, on his ranch at present Sussex, Wyoming, where Salt Creek joins Powder River, ten miles east of Kaycee. Ernie eventually bought the Davis ranch, and still owned it late in his life when he and Nola bought the Bar C.

The Vests, therefore, never thought of the Bar C as their home place, their eighty-four year old daughter Arlene "Tat" Vest Yeigh remembers now. Her mother and father more or less camped there, Tat says—meaning they stayed in a trailer or in one of the cabins when they were on the place. They ran cattle on both ranches, with the best hay ground on the lower ranch. More than a few times, Tat remembers, she and her husband Rex trailed cattle horseback from the lower ranch all the way to the Bar C, and up on the mountain to leased summer range.

In 1965, the fabulous Reno oil field was discovered on the Vests' lower ranch. Ernie by then had modest oil properties—but this one was substantial. It was paying out twenty-eight thousand dollars a month to the Vests when Ernie died in 1967, Tat remembers now. Still, the characterization of Ernie as a person who started out a dirt-poor cowboy and died an oil-rich rancher is far too simple a picture of an interesting man, Tat says. "My dad was a common man. If you'd have seen him in town, the way he dressed, you'd never have known he [owned the oil field]."

One of the best things Ernie did, says Tat, was to sell a right-of-way to the Bureau of Land Management so that the public, in perpetuity, could drive through the Bar C to the public land on the mountain, where the Middle Fork flows through Outlaw Canyon. For many years a sign at the Bar C commemorated the permanent right of way. After it was taken down, Tat said, she felt a little offended. Still, she admitted, all that new public access brought new pressures on the ranch. Fisherman would sneak down through the canyon and turn up fishing right behind the Bar C barn, strewing garbage wherever they went.

The ranches and their obligations fell immediately on the family when Ernie died in October 1967. Tat quit her job so she could help out with fall weaning and shipping. Her mother, Nola, took over running the ranch, and for part of the time Tat's son, Gary Yeigh, lived on and worked the Bar C.

Ernie liked to let his friends fish on the ranch, but not too many; he had fishing-permission cards made to ward off confusion. Among these fishermen was John Wold. Tat remembers she once lent him an old pair of Rex's pants, after John fell in the river.

But gradually Nola turned her interests elsewhere. She and one of her grandsons went into the racehorse business, first in Arizona and then in Montrose, Colorado, without great results. She sold the lower ranch in 1974. In 1980, she sold the Bar C, back to the Culvers—and the Gosmans, and the Wolds, in a three-way deal. Since then, says Tat, the Wolds have done a wonderful job with the place. The Vests' lower ranch, she said, has not fared so well.

"When you sell a place, you love it, and to see somebody improve it is just great," she said.[27]

# The Wolds, Culvers, and Gosmans

In the early 1960s, when Peter Wold was still in grade school in Casper, his father, John, would take him to the Bar C to fish the Spring Creek beaver ponds. They'd use Mepps spinners, but it was still just as crucial—as it would be later with a fly—that your first cast be a good one. "You'd throw in, and all of a sudden you'd see this pond, kind of, lurch. And you'd see this big submarine below the surface, this wave following your lure."

Sometimes John would take Nola Vest a crate of oranges or grapefruit in thanks, or a fifth of whiskey. Handing it over, he'd add, "If you're ever interested in selling the ranch, let me know."

By the 1970s, the Wolds remember, Nola was mostly running yearlings. She would bring in a thousand of them in the spring, turn them loose on the ranch, sell them and ship them out in the fall. But her true interest by then was racing horses, not ranching. In 1980 she called John. Was he still interested?

But the Vests had also given the Culvers a verbal right of first refusal all the way back in 1961, when Ernie Vest had bought the ranch from Elizabeth Culver. And since that time the Vests had allowed the Culvers to continue fishing on the place.

The Culvers often brought along their friends the Gosmans. Bob Gosman, an exploration geologist, first came to Wyoming in 1959, and worked for Warren Morton. Later he went into the bottled-gas business with his good friend Jerry Culver. From his earliest summers in the state, Bob had loved to fish the Middle Fork through Outlaw Canyon. Even better was a chance to fish the stretch of river running through the ranch.

Nola and John Wold roughed out a price, and Nola approached Jerry about it at the same time. Eventually, Nola worked out a deal with the Culvers, Gosmans, and Wolds. Culvers and Gosmans would buy the downstream part of the ranch, east of the BLM road, about thirteen hundred acres. The Wolds would buy the rest, and Wolds, Culvers, and Gosmans agreed to divide up the price on a per-acre basis.

Peter Wold remembers walking on the road with his dad, Jerry Culver, and Bob Gosman, when John asked the other two men if they'd prefer to buy a forty-acre, or perhaps an eighty-acre piece. They wanted the land primarily for the fishing, after all. So the two walked off to talk about it, and returned in fifteen minutes. They wanted to stick with the original idea. The Wolds said fine, but said they would also like to carve out of the downstream, eastern half enough for the house and corrals on that side, as they planned to run cows and would need a ranch headquarters. So to the Wolds' half was added 120 acres more, east of the road—with the manager's house, which they enlarged, corrals, and an existing barn.

For their price the Wolds got about sixteen hundred deeded acres, and a lot of federal leases and a little bit of state. The recession of the early eighties soon followed, oil prices dropped, and the uranium business more or less disappeared. Nola was a shrewd bargainer. The Wolds knew they'd bought at the top of the market.

In 1981 the Wolds bought land on the mountain slopes west of the Bar C headquarters from a Casper airline pilot named George Taylor. No relation to the Taylors of the Blue Creek Ranch, he owned the Willow Creek Ranchsouth of the Bar C.

In a three-way swap under provision 1031 of the federal tax code, John Wold sold his majority interest in a uranium property, the Christiansen Ranch, to Arizona Public Service. That utility bought George Taylor's mountain ranch property, and then traded it to John for partial payment for the uranium interests.

Around this time, the Wolds remodeled the old barn, adding a second floor for dances. But on the Fourth of July, the ranch manager, a smoker, was sharpening a blade on an old grindstone in a shed attached to the barn—probably the same grindstone the Hartnett women remembered from when they were girls. A spark caught in the hay, or somewhere, and the barn caught quickly. The Wolds were at a celebration on Mark Gordon's Hat Ranch, on the North Fork, when they got the phone call; Gosmans and Culvers were celebrating at a gazebo picnic shelter they'd built on the lower end of their property. County fire trucks came, but by then the road was crowded with neighbors and rubberneckers, and no one could save the barn.

Next the Wolds bought a connecting piece on Poker Creek, from Curt Taylor of the Blue Creek ranch. This piece, which includes nice bass ponds and a big set of corrals where the Wolds now brand, lies south of the original Bar C. The next piece the Wolds bought was on Sheep Creek, north and east of the Gosmans' and Culvers' piece—this time from Garvin Taylor, also of the Blue Creek Taylors. It was about twelve hundred acres, tying the mountain land together with the lower slopes. The parcel included the house on what's now the lowest end of the ranch, part of Castle Rock, and the Sheep Creek pond, a great swimming hole. A lease on a state section came with the purchase.

The Gosmans and Culvers, meanwhile, settled in to enjoy their half of the ranch. Bob Gosman and his wife Barbara fished from daylight to dark every summer weekend for years, starting at the bottom end of the ranch and fishing all the way up to the mouth of Outlaw Canyon, scrambling over rocks and hills in their rubber boots, keeping a few trout to eat and throwing the rest back.

The two families built the gazebo about a mile downstream from where the county road crosses the Middle Fork. Later they built two cabins along the river, east of the main road, and Culvers built a small house across the river from the gazebo. For a while they leased the grazing on their parcel to Wayne Graves, who ranches north of Barnum, and later to Ross Buckingham, who lived up on the slope. But after a while they felt the cattle were damaging the land along the creek, and stopped the practice. They were there primarily to fish.

The Gosmans remember those years fondly. Their grandchildren loved the place, loved fishing, tubing, and scrambling on the slopes and rocks. They remember mountain lions on the rocks, too—and once was in the gazebo and another turned up on the back porch of the Gosmans' cabin.

In the mid-1980s, the state got serious about the proposal

to dam the Middle Fork at a spot two miles downstream from the east end of the ranch. The dam would have backed water all the way up to the bridge over the Middle Fork on the BLM road.

"Our meadows out there would have been a shallow lake at high water; at low water a dirty, ugly mud flat. And the creek would have been destroyed," Bob Gosman says now. Together with the Wolds, and other neighbors like Graveses and Harlans, the Gosmans began lobbying against the dam, bringing legislators and state water commissioners out to the ranch for a look.

The proposal finally went away after Exxon was no longer interested in the water; water prices that irrigators could afford would never have financed the dam. And legislators got cold feet once they learned the cost of the archeology that would have to have been done before construction could even begin; the Middle Fork proved rich in ancient sites.[28]

During these years, the long tradition of distinguished visitors to the ranch continued. Among them was U.S. Congressman, later Secretary of Defense Dick Cheney, (and much later, vice president.) Cheney is a longtime friend of John Wold, and managed to find time to come to the ranch once every four or five years, for the fishing.

Not long after the first Gulf War, Cheney made it known he'd like to come up and bring his wife, Lynne, with him. The Wolds made arrangements, Jack Wold remembers now. Members of the Secret Service came a week ahead of time, to check out the ranch, see what the security needs would be, and make sure satellite communications would work. On the way in they mistakenly stopped at the Harlan ranch, about ten miles downstream from the Bar C. There they were directed properly. But their stop meant that it was no longer much of a secret in Johnson County that somebody important was likely to arrive

Dick Cheney loves to fish, and visited the Bar C
a number of times during his years of public service.
Left to right: John Wold, Mary Cheney, Jack Wold,
Dick Cheney, and Peter Wold at the ranch in May 1989.
*Wold family photo.*

behind the Red Wall, pretty soon.

The following week, when the secretary arrived, he stayed at the Wolds' house on the ranch. The secret servicemen stayed at the house of the Richendifers, who managed the ranch then as now. Cheney loves to fish and he's good at it, Jack Wold says now. The first day, he was already out on the Middle Fork when a Wyoming game warden arrived, to welcome Mr. Cheney—but also to check his license.

At Richendifers' the warden had a long conversation with the secret servicemen. They assured him Cheney always wore his license inside an envelope of clear plastic, pinned to the front of his fishing vest. There was no need, they assured the warden, for him to check any further.

But the warden, according to Jack, said, "you know, guys, that doesn't do it." He went and got in his truck, spotted the secretary of defense on the stream, and drove toward him. Only at this point, according to Jack, did it dawn on the secret servicemen that an armed man was approaching their charge. Game wardens in Wyoming are law enforcement officers, and carry pistols on the job.

The warden jumped out of his truck and confronted the secretary of defense, who was quite cheerful. Cheney showed the license on the front of his vest as advertised, and said he'd worn it the day before, too, when he was fishing near Thermopolis. The conversation was civil, even friendly on both sides, and the warden left, closely followed by the secret service.

Afterward, the secret servicemen said it was the first time, in travels with Cheney all over the world, that any local law enforcement agent had questioned their judgment about anything.

The Wolds were distressed at how their guest had been

treated. "Dad expressed some dissatisfaction, and the secret servicemen were shocked and stunned that their judgment and assurances were questioned and ignored. This violated the unwritten code of law enforcement officers of accepting the word and trust of a fellow officer," Jack says now.

Later, the game warden was transferred from Kaycee to the Wind River Reservation. There's no doubt, Jack says, that the warden was acting entirely within his job description. But Cheney came to the ranch for "peace, calm, and quiet," and it was unfortunate that that quiet was disturbed, Jack says.[29]

As the years passed, the Gosman and Culver grandchildren got older and visited less; their grandparents got older, too, and caring for the place became more difficult. Then Jerry Culver died, and Bonnie Culver decided she wanted to sell. But the two families had never divided their half; they'd never had to. Bob Gosman realized the simplest thing was for him to sell too, and he was ready, in any case.

"They put a hell of a price tag on it," Peter Wold says now. John Wold by this time was eighty-nine, and felt he had other things to do with his money. So Peter and his brother Jack bought Gosmans' undivided half of the property, and then made a separate deal with Bonnie Culver.

Last they bought what they now describe as the Doornbos parcel. When George Taylor of the Willow Creek Ranchsold the mountain land in the 1980s, he separated it into three pieces, of which the Wolds bought two. Taylor sold the third piece to Casper businessman Phil Doornbos and several friends who owned an oil company in Wichita. The friends owned eighty-five percent of the company; Phil owned the rest. When he died, he left money in his will for a nephew to buy out the friends' eighty-five percent interest in the land. The nephew preferred cash, however, which meant the best solution was for him to buy out the friends with his legacy, and then sell the entire parcel. To make *that* possible, he needed a willing buyer.

A Jackson lawyer contacted the Wolds on behalf of the Doornbos estate, and they agreed to the deal. The nephew also negotiated a lifetime right to hunt and fish on the property. "Nice guy," says Peter. "He's been up once since the deal. Lives in Kansas." There's a big trailer on the land, plus a cabin with a spring among pines and aspen.

In 2006, the Wolds changed the name from Bar C Ranch to Hole in the Wall Ranch, finding the new name better expresses the fame and the history of the whole region. The Wolds have held the ranch now for thirty years—longer than any other owner, and more than twice as long as any of the owners except Alex Cunningham, who had it for about twenty-two years.[30]

And the Richendifers have run the ranch for the Wolds most of that time. In July 1986, Jim Richendifer, his wife Kerri, and their young children Seth, Kyra, and Zach arrived on the ranch. The children grew up there and attended Kaycee schools. Zach, after some years at college and working construction, returned to the ranch in November 2007—and his parents are glad of the help, Jim Richendifer says now. It's a big job, with a herd of eight hundred mother cows, their calves, and, in 2010, 128 yearlings. The Richendifers buy Angus bulls from the Van Dyke Angus Ranch in Manhattan, Montana, and have built a herd that thrives on the rough mix of mountain, canyon, and valley country that makes up the Hole in the Wall Ranch today. Richendifers have now lived and worked the ranch nearly a quarter century, longer than any other operators since the ranch was founded.[31]

Beginning in the 1980s, the Wolds enlarged and improved the house at the ranch headquarters where the Richendifers live.

Wold family and friends–shown here in 2008–gather at the Hole in the Wall Ranch every April for Branding. *Bruce Nichols photo.*

After the old barn burned, they built a new one on the rise south of the ranch house. When Zack returned to work full time on the ranch, he moved into what had been the Culvers' house, a mile or so downstream and across the river from the gazebo. And for themselves, the Wolds have built a comfortable house near where Spring Creek cuts in under the buffalo-jump bluff.

# The Wolds

John Wold, his wife Jane, their children Peter Wold, Jack Wold, and Priscilla Wold Longfield, their children's spouses, and their children's children all seem to have a deep love for the place and its history. The Wolds love Wyoming too, and have made generous contributions over the years of their time, energy, money, and know-how to its well being. By taking care of the ranch, they also understand they are caring for an important piece of Wyoming's history—and by doing so, making yet another contribution to the future of the state.

Every spring, the Wolds and Richendifers brand around seven hundred Angus calves, with the help of a crowd of other friends, neighbors, grandchildren, and grandchildren's friends. The brand is a version of the one Peters and Alston began with, in 1881.

A big, framed map of Peters' and Alston's holdings hangs on the back wall of the Hoofprints of the Past Museum, in

Kaycee. The map dates from the 1880s, and shows their land claims around the confluence of Buffalo Creek and the Middle Fork. It also shows a great deal more country, running north, south, east and west, with the implication that their cattle ranged in those directions. The same would have been true of Bar C owners for fifty more years. Cattle and sheep ranged on a mix of private and public land, but who got to use which tracts of public land was a mix of local custom, competition, and geography. The situation didn't really change until the passage of the Taylor Grazing Act in 1934, which set up a formal system of federal grazing leases, attached to specific ranches. State land leasing runs on a similar system. When pieces of deeded land are sold, the leases attached to it generally go along with the sale.

As a result, the ranch has never stayed one size or shape for long; the present ranch boundaries are the result of a hundred years of land deals, plus thirty years of the Wolds' assembling pieces as they became available.

From a spot on the Middle Fork of Powder River about three miles northeast—downstream—from the headquarters, the ranch boundary now runs south along the east side of Buffalo Creek about six miles, past the Bar C Gap and past where Poker Creek joins Buffalo Creek, to the southeast corner of the ranch. The line then jogs west six miles, south for three, then west again, climbing all the way to the Hazelton Road, which runs along the crest of the Bighorns for forty miles or more. From here the boundary runs north for some miles, then back east, down slope, parallel now to the deep canyon of the Middle Fork, and crosses the river at one of the canyon's deepest spots. Now the ranch border skirts a state section, and begins jogging north and east, back out into the flats along Sheep Creek, past Castle Rock and nearly all the way to Barnum, and back around another state section to the northeast corner of the ranch. From the northeast corner southwest to the tip that touches the Hazelton Road must be something like fifteen miles. The acres total around forty-five thousand, a third of which is deeded land, half is federal grazing leases, and the rest state leases.

It makes for a spectacular variety of country—hay meadows and winter grazing along the creeks and the lower stretches, summer range on the mountain, sagebrush, juniper, high, grassy expanses, deep and sudden limestone canyons. Summer and fall the public is welcome to drive through the ranch up to the BLM campground, on top of a limestone cliff looking right down into the Middle Fork Canyon at its deepest point. A steep trail takes fishermen down to the river. Outlaw Cave, supposedly a hideout once, is just across the river; old photos show cowboys at its mouth, forted up with miscellaneous planks. The Wolds cooperate with the state Game and Fish Department and the BLM in maintaining other fishing access spots, too, and in protecting crucial elk winter range in the Ed O. Taylor Habitat Management Area just outside the ranch boundary, along the Middle Fork Canyon.

Splendid vistas open up around every corner. One of the best is from the top of the buffalo-jump bluff. Here a person can look far up the valley and down, with the Red Wall stretching along the eastern rim of things and the mountain rising in its even grade to the west. Ancient people must have stood here just to look—and tribal people, trapping people, and traveling people—some pressed to their limits and others blessed with what felt like limitless time.

The Frewens, Alston, and Peters would have passed by more than once with well-dressed parties of English swells. Surely Nate Champion came up here for the view, too, and maybe the men who were out to kill him that November morning rode over the bluff this way, hunting for his cabin door. Surely Lizzie Lea climbed up here, to long for a better life. Charles and Martha King came up here, and Ada and Alex Cunningham, and young Joe Burke, and the Cronin brothers, the Baxters, Hartnetts, Culvers, their tenant Jack Greer, the Vests, Culvers again, and Gosmans, and plenty of Wolds.

Boundaries can preserve a place like this—unique, diverse, and frankly glorious—for a very long time. They make the ranch a base for imagining the future, thanks to the stories it preserves from a long and vivid past.

*Bruce Nichols photo.*

The Wold family at the Hole in the Wall Ranch, 2001. Left to right: Holly Wold, Jack Wold, Allison Wold, Hildy Wold, Court Wold, Cecily Longfield, John Wold, Jane Wold, Matt Wold, Marla Wold, Peter Wold, Claire Longfield, Abbie Wold, Priscilla W. Longfield, John Longfield, Joe Wold. *Wold family photo.*

*Notes*

## Chapter 1: Beginnings

[1] Mokler, *History of Natrona County*, 314; Urbanek, *Wyoming Place Names*, 103: Hanson, ed. *Powder River Country*, 407; Condit, "The Hole-in-the-Wall: Part 1, Location and Origin of Name."

[2] Rea, *Bone Wars*, 172-175; interview with Mike Flynn, retired Sheridan College geology instructor, 1/15/10. These finds deepened the museum crews' understanding of the animal's anatomy just as they were assembling a full-sized *Diplodocus* cast, a gift from Andrew Carnegie to the King of England.

[3] Francis, "Three Rock Art Sites on the Middle Fork of the Powder River, Wyoming," *Archaeology in Montana*, 28:2, 1987, p. 19, and telephone conversations, 12/18/08 and 1/26/09.

4 Missouri Basin Project, "Appraisal of the Archaeological and Paleontological Resources of the Middle Fork Area, Johnson County, Wyoming." Smithsonian Institution, Washington, D.C., 1953.

5 Unsigned article, probably Glenn Sweem, "The Sweem-Taylor Site, 48 JO 301," *Wyoming Archaeologist*, II:10, November, 1959, pp. 4-8. Glenn Sweem and Don Grey, "The Sweem-Taylor Site, 48 JO 301." Draft of ca. 1960 article in Sweem manuscript collection, now in possession of Scott Burgan, Sheridan, Wyoming.

6 Julie Francis, "The Middle Fork of the Powder River: 1947-1985." *North Dakota Archaeology*, vol. 5, 1994, pp. 177-189.

7 Albanese, John, and Allen Darlington, William Eckerle, and Julie Francis. "48JO966: A New Bison Jump Site From the East Flank of the Bighorn Mountains, Johnson County, Wyoming." Paper presented at the 42nd Plains Archeology Conference, Iowa City, Iowa. October 1985.

8 Loendorf, Larry, and Julie Francis. "Three Rock Art Sites on the Middle Fork of the Powder River, Wyoming." *Archaeology in Montana*, 28:2, 1987, 18-24.

9 Francis, "Middle Fork," 180-82, and personal conversations, 12/18/08 and 1/26/09.

## Chapter 2: Crow and Cheyenne Country

1 McCleary, *The Stars We Know*, 16-18

2 Larocque's is almost certainly the first description of Powder River ever written down, and, for the lower stretch he was on, remains accurate: "The current in that river is very strong and the water so muddy as to be hardly drinkable. The Indians sai [sic] it is always so,

and that is the reason they call it Powder River, from the great quantity of drifting fine sand set in motion by the Const[ant] wind which blinds people and dirtys the water. There are very large sand shoals along the river for several acres breadth and length. The bed of the River is likewise sand, and its course North East." Larocque in Wood and Thiessen, *Early Fur Trade on the Northern Plains*, 178. Another author quotes Edward Bennett, early settler of Johnson County, Wyoming, who said the Indian sign for Powder River was to "pick up a pinch of dust and blow on it, also [to] sign 'very crooked.'" Frink, *Cow Country Cavalcade*, 20.

3 Wood and Thiessen, 206.

4 Lamar, ed. in Stuart, *The Discovery of the Oregon Trail: Robert Stuart's Narratives of his Overland Trip Eastward from Astoria in 1812-13*. Edited by Philip Ashton Rollins. New York: Scribner's Sons, 1935, pp. v-vi.

5 Many of these stories were written down by U.S. Army Capt. Reuben Holmes, a West Point graduate who met Rose at treaty negotiations at the Mandan villages in 1825. See Holmes, "The Five Scalps."

6 Hunt in Stuart, 281.

7 Hunt, in Stuart, 284-285; 315 n. 100.

8 Philip Ashton Rollins, who edited Hunt's journals in 1935, on Hunt's route, in Stuart, p. 315, n. 95.

9 Rev. J. Neilson Barry, "The Trail of the Astorians." *The Quarterly of the Oregon Historical Society*, xiii:3, September 1912, p. 231

10 Bureau of Land Management archaeologists B.J. Earle (Buffalo) and Mike Bies (Worland), interviews, March 2009.

[11] Hanson, ed., *Powder River Country*, 3-7. Frison, Paul. *Calendar of Change*. Worland, Wyoming: Serlkay, Inc., 1975, p. 22; Condit, 28; Brock Hanson telephone conversation, Sept. 13, 2009.

[12] Thelma Gatchell Condit, "The Hole-in-the-Wall: Part 2—The Indians," *Annals of Wyoming*, 28:1 April 1956. p. 25; Frison, 22-23; H.M. Chittenden, *The American Fur Trade of the Far West*, Stanford, California: Academic Reprints, 1954. v. 2, 197. Chittenden, whose classic history of the fur trade was first published in 1902, knew Wyoming topography well. He discussed the Astorians' likely route over the Bighorns with former Wyoming Governor W.A. Richards, who owned a ranch on Little Canyon Creek and was, Chittenden says, "a close student of the history of his state."

[13] Hunt in Stuart, 285-86

[14] In 1833, a trapper named Zenas Leonard found an "old negro" in a big Crow village at the confluence of the Bighorn and Stinking Water (now Shoshone) rivers, enjoying high status and four wives. The man spoke Crow fluently, had been in the country since the time of Lewis and Clark, and was looked to as a leader in war and peace. It had to have been Edward Rose. Leonard, *Narrative of the Adventures of Zenas Leonard...; written by himself.* The mountain man Jim Beckwourth, also part African American, likewise lived many years among the Crow but would have been young in 1833, not old. Another story has Rose killed by Arickaras on an ice-covered Yellowstone 1828. Still another story is implied in the name of a wood station for steamboats far up the Missouri near the mouth of Milk River—Rose's Grave. Blenkinsop, "Edward Rose," 345. Berry, *A Majority of Scoundrels*, 371, argues that the mountain men "who became Indians in name as well as in fact," never trying to rejoin Euro-American society after the fur trade ended, were the ones who died happiest.

15 Utley, 12

16 Denig, *Five Indian Tribes of the Upper Missouri*, 169-170. This may have been the same epidemic that hit the central Plains in 1831 and was stopped from moving farther up the Missouri by a U.S. government inoculation effort. See Michael K. Trimble, "The 1832 Inoculation Programs on the Missouri River," in Verano and Ubelaker, eds, *Disease and Demography in the Americas*, Washington: Smithsonian Institution Press, 1992, pp. 257-264.

17 Gary Peterson "Antonio Montero and the Portuguese Houses: An Outpost on Powder River." *Rocky Mountain Fur Trade Journal* vol. 2, 2008, 31-47. pp. 37-39.

18 Peterson, 40-41. Peterson's source for Bridger's whereabouts the winter of 1836-37 is the mountain man Joe Meek, in Frances Fuller Victor, *The River of the West: The Adventures of Joe Meek*, vol. 1 (Missoula: Mountain Press Publishing Company, 1983), 223-24. Meek is more reliable for flavor than fact, especially for dates, but DeVoto, *Across the Wide Missouri*, 271, seems to at least partially corroborate that Bridger and his brigade wintered on Powder River that year. These large brigades routinely included trappers' families— usually Indian wives and mixed-race children—so a more traditionally sized brigade of 60 or 70 trappers could easily have come to 300 people. See Utley, *A Life Wild and Perilous*, 86, for more on brigades and how they worked.

Bridger's Rocky Mountain Fur Company was defunct by this time, and the famous trapper was employed by the American Fur Company. Just a few years earlier, American Fur Company traders at Fort Cass at the mouth of the Bighorn River used Crows to steal everything valuable from a brigade led by the Rocky Mountain Fur Company's Tom Fitzpatrick; Bridger here seems to be using the Crows for a similar purpose against Montero—and thus against Bonneville, the last main AFC competitor east of the Divide. See Berry, *Majority of*

*Scoundrels*, 334-336 and 366-68.

[19] Robertson, *Rotting Face*, 254.

[20] Denig 186 n. 35, and *Annual Report of the Commissioner of Indian Affairs, 1853*, 354.

[21] See "Ethnographic Setting" at:
http://lib.lbhc.cc.mt.us/about/genealogy/kinship2.php as of 4.21.10.

[22] Doyle, *Journeys to the Land of Gold*, 65-66.

[23] Condit, "The Hole in the Wall, Part 2—the Indians;" Greene, *Morning Star Dawn*; Hanson, ed., *Powder River Country*, 88-107; Smith, *Sagebrush Soldier*; Stands in Timber and Liberty, *Cheyenne Memories*, 214-217; Warner, *The Dull Knife Battle*.

## Chapter 3: The British Come to Hole in the Wall

[1] Brayer, "The 76 Ranch on Powder River," 73-74; Condit "The Big Cow Outfits," 41-43; David, *Malcolm Campbell*, 69; Frewen, *Melton Mowbray*, 146-148; Lott, ed. "Major Wise Diary," 87-88, n.4 and 90-91, n. 6; Woods, *Moreton Frewen's Western Adventures*, 19-25.

[2] Lott, ed. "Major Wise Diary," 89-90, n.6

[3] Digby, *Plunkett*, 21-24, 27. He wore ordinary cowboy duds, too—hat, chaps, kerchief, checked shirt—not as a costume but as work clothes on the ranch.

[4] Savage, *Sir Horace Plunkett in Wyoming*, 8-10.

[5] Savage, 27.

6 David, *Malcolm Campbell*, 70-71. The biggest herd reported by Frewen's Powder River Cattle Company was 54,581 at the end of 1884. The company's actual calf brand and sales figures that year suggest strongly that the number was inflated. The figure almost certainly came from a book count, a common estimating process at the time. Ranchers extrapolated from previous herd sizes using projected rates of increase and loss. Woods, *Frewen's Adventures*, 117.

7 Frewen married Clara Jerome, aunt of the future Winston Churchill, in 1881. From the start, however, Clara had a difficult time in Wyoming. The long coach ride from Rock Creek on the Union Pacific Railroad to Powder River exhausted her badly. Still, dozens of aristocratic guests soon followed her to the ranche, and were still on hand some weeks later when she announced to Moreton that she was pregnant. Everyone celebrated, but on a trip to the mountains she fell ill. The journey back to the railroad was even more difficult than before, and in Cheyenne she miscarried. Moreton and his sister Louise traveled with her back to New York. She never returned to Powder River. Woods, *Frewen's Adventures*, 55.

8 Smith, 12.

9 *Cheyenne Democratic Leader*, July 9, 1885; *Cheyenne Daily Sun*, July 31, 1885; *Cheyenne Democratic Leader*, Oct. 16, 1886; *Cheyenne Daily Sun*, Sept. 9, 1887.

10 Lott, Howard B., ed. "Diary of Major Wise, Hunting Trip in Powder River Country in 1880." *Annals of Wyoming* vol. 12, no. 2, April 1940, pp. 85-118. Hanna was the first white settler of the town of Big Horn, near present Sheridan. Frank Boughton was probably a relative of Plunkett's partner Edward Boughton. See Savage, *Cattle King*, 24, 26. Lott, 114, n.24, says Peters was a Philadelphian, and later a U.S. consul in Germany. Condit and Woods say he was English. Cheyenne papers in the 1880s note his occasional arrivals from or

departures to Philadelphia or "the East," and a notice published in 1917 says he died in Germantown, Pa. See *Cheyenne Daily Leader*, July 11, 1882 and May 5, 1883; *Cheyenne Daily Sun*, Nov. 1, 1887; *Buffalo Bulletin* March 1, 1917.

[11] Condit, "The Big Cow Outfits," 50-55, and Devoe, "Some Reminiscences." These stories and Wise's hunt diary from 1880 may show the southern Bighorns as one of the last places where buffalo were fairly plentiful.

[12] Smith, *The War on Powder River*, 94 n.

[13] Condit, "Cow outfits," 52-53.

[14] Geoffrey Millais to his mother, June 21, 1885 and Aug. 13, 1886; G.M. to his Uncle George (no last name given) July 31, 1886; Geoffrey Millais to his father, John Millais, June 2, no year given, probably 1885 or '86. American Heritage Center. Johnnie Millais later became a well-known ornithologist and painter of birds.

[15] Geoffrey Millais to his father, June 2, no year. American Heritage Center.

[16] Geoffrey Millais to his mother, Aug. 22, 1884, AHC. In 1883, when everything looked rosy, Horace Plunkett, his partner E.S.R. Boughton, Alston, and Millais, threw a party at the Cheyenne Club for 32 club members. Sixty-six bottles of champagne and 20 of red wine were consumed by the celebrants, more than two and a half bottles per guest. "I never saw such a cordial drunk. Everyone was drunk. No one beastly drunk. The singing and speaking were humorous and good," Plunkett wrote afterward. The next year, when the Americans tried to return the favor, Plunkett judged it an edgy failure, with everyone drunk before dinner even started. Woods, *British Gentlemen*, 148-149.

[17] Brayer, "The 76 Ranch on Powder River," 75-77, and Woods, *British Gentlemen*, 84-89. The Earl of Wharncliffe's, nephew, Ralph Stuart-Wortley, soon joined Millais in investing with Alston and Peters.

[18] Brayer, 75; Woods, *British Gentlemen,* 84-85.

[19] Woods, *Frewen's Adventures,* 89.

[20] Woods, *Frewen's Adventures*, 67-68, 89, 123-124, 128-136. Murphy was in fact fired a number of times, but kept getting his job back as lines of authority in the company were so unclear.

[21] Woods, *Frewen's Adventures*, 138-148

[22] Digby, *Plunkett*, 35.

[23] Smith, *The War on Powder River*, 32-33.

[24] WSGA executive committee minutes, July 20 and August 2, 1886, AHC; Smith, 32-33. Jack Flagg and some others ended up blackballed in any case, with consequences that led directly to the feuds of 1892. In some circles the moderate Thomas Willing "Twice Wintered" Peters was also known as "Too Willing" Peters, for being too willing to pay his cowboys well. (Casper) *Wyoming Derrick*, Feb. 19. 1903, p. 1.

[25] Woods, *Frewen's Adventures*, 182. Plunkett was always ambivalent about Americans, however. "They don't like us naturally, and we on a whole don't like them," he wrote in his diary. "They are to a certain amount clannish, and feel our intrusion. The exact feeling they would express thus. 'You have a social position, we have hardly any. You compare us with your society. We don't compare favourably, perhaps. But we are a greater nation than yours and just as good as though you didn't know it." Digby, *Plunkett*, 28, gives no date for the diary entry.

[26] Woods, *Frewen's Adventures*, 184, *British Gentlemen*, 173, and personal communication, 5/14/09; *Cheyenne Daily Leader*, Oct. 10, 1890.

## Chapter 4: Rustler Heaven

[1] McDermott, Fred. "A Misunderstood Term." Interview of Fred McDermott of Glendo, Wyoming, ca. 1938, by Minnie Rietz. Wyoming State Archives, WPA file #899, p. 3; Smith, "The Truth about the Hole-in-the-Wall Fight," 13.

[2] Smith, *War on Powder River*, 154-155; N.D. Champion to B.F. Champion, March 2 and April 16, 1891, Johnson County Library archives.

[3] A few years later Barnum, where Blue Creek joins Beaver Creek, became the official post office and remained a community center down to the present.

[4] Wister, *Owen Wister Out West*, 102-113. Wister used this event in his short story, "Balaam and Pedro," and again in *The Virginian*, published in 1902.

[5] David, *Malcolm Campbell, Sheriff*, 128-129; Smith, *War on Powder River*, 153-154.

[6] The Wold family had this cabin reconstructed on the north side of the Middle Fork about a quarter mile downstream from the mouth of the canyon, at a spot where a foundation and parts of a chimney remained from an earlier structure. In July 2004 the Wolds staged a public re-enactment of the attack on Champion to celebrate the history of the area. The reconstructed cabin burned in the big Middle Fork forest fire of August 2006. Casper resident Colin Taylor, relative of the Stubbses and Taylors of the Blue Creek ranch, says the Hall

cabin was in fact on the south side of the river. (Colin Taylor interview, September 16, 2009.) Lizzie Lea Rawson remembered a dance the winter of 1899-1900, given by Joe Williams, who lived in a tiny cabin near the canyon mouth—probably the old Hall cabin. The dance was a housewarming for a new "very nice two-roomed log house" Williams had just finished building nearby. Perhaps the old cabin and the new house were on opposite sides of the Middle Fork. (Rawson, Elizabeth Lea. *Looking for the End of the Rainbow*, 155-56.)

[7] Colin Taylor interview, September 16, 2009

[8] Glenn Sweem oral history 4/22/96, transcript p. 2. Sweem's story, contrary to published accounts, implies there were five men in the attack, and one was killed. Or perhaps four attacked the cabin, and the fifth man was Shonsey. The ex-stage guard had returned to the Bar C that summer to visit old haunts. He still worked as a security guard in a Los Angeles department store. Colin Taylor says the man shot was Billy Lykens. Burroughs, *Guardians*, p. 115, agrees that may have been true.

[9] The best contemporary source on the subject, biased and spirited, is A.S. Mercer, *The Banditti of the Plains*. The best book overall remains *The War on Powder River*, by Helena Huntington Smith, published in 1966. The most recent as of this writing is *The Johnson County War* by Bill O'Neal, which includes new information on the Texans. Due out soon, as of this writing, is John W. Davis' *Wyoming Range War*, which shines a spotlight on the invaders' claim that convictions of rustlers had become impossible in Johnson County.

[10] Smith, *The War on Powder River*, 252-259, 282-83; Schubert, Frank N., "The Suggs Affray: The Black Cavalry in the Johnson County War." Western Historical Quarterly, January 1973, pp. 57-68; Hanson, ed. *Powder River Country*, 476-477.

[11] Nicholas, Liza J. *Becoming Western: Stories of Culture and Identity in the Cowboy State.* Lincoln: University of Nebraska Press, 2006, 1-32.

[12] Patterson, *Butch Cassidy: A Biography*, 23-53.

[13] Curt Taylor, in *Our Powder River Heritage*, 219-221.

[14] Johnson County land records. Other local tradition names Brown Parker the earliest settler on Blue Creek. A cultured if profane easterner, he ran the Riverside Post office and had a prosperous ranch going there by 1892, the year of the Invasion. Part of the Cassidy confusion must stem from this man's name. The ditch on the Blue Creek Ranch is still known as Brown Parker ditch. Anita Webb Deininger to Bill Jones, March 18, 1976, citing notes she took after a conversation with Tommy Carr in 1955, Tisdale Collection, Hole in the Wall file, Johnson County Library.

[15] Kelly, *The Outlaw Trail*, 116-118; Lamb, *The Wild Bunch*, 81-83; "The State Press," *Saratoga Sun*, October 17, 1895, p. 4, introduced the idea of stock thieves around Hole-in-the-Wall as if both the concept and the geography were new to its readers; see also *Crook County Monitor*, October 30, 1895, p. 4; and Buffalo *Bulletin*, October 31, 1895, p. 3. Flat-nosed George Currie is not to be confused with Big-nosed George Parrott, who was lynched in downtown Rawlins in March 1881. Harvey Logan also used the aliases Kid Curry and Harve Ray; he should also not be confused with Nick Ray, who died with Champion at the KC Ranch.

[16] Smith, "The Truth about the Hole-in-the-Wall Fight," 13, and *War on Powder River*, 252-259; Wister, Owen Wister Out West, 106, 117-118; Colin Taylor, interview, 9/16/09.

[17] Saratoga Sun, Sept. 10, 1896, p. 4.

18 Divine letters, 1897, in Hanson, ed. *Powder River Country*, 429-434.

19 Hanson, ed., *Powder River Country*, 435-436.

20 *Ibid.*, 440.

21 Patterson, 125-127; Lamb, *The Wild Bunch*, 114-115.

22 Ogallala Ranch cattle generally ran well east of Powder River, on Antelope Creek in Converse County. Burroughs, *Guardians*, 184-185. The Pugsleys were on Meadow Creek in Converse County. Mokler, 115.

23 Smith, "The Truth about the Hole-in-the-Wall Fight," 13-16; "Bob Smith Killed," Buffalo Bulletin, July 29, 1897, p. 2; "Desperate Bloody Fight," Natrona County Tribune, July 29, 1897; "Bob Smith Killed," Buffalo Bulletin, July 29, 1897, p. 2; Burroughs, *Guardian of the Grasslands*, 191-195; Colin Taylor interview with Charlie Firnekas, September 7 and 8, 2002, copy supplied by interviewer. Charlie Firnekas' father was a good friend of Bob Taylor, and always maintained it was LeFors, and not Divine, who shot Bob Smith in the back.

24 Smith, "The Truth about the Hole-in-the-Wall Fight," 16-19.

25 "'Brave Bob Devine' Again." *Crook County Monitor* (Sundance, Wyo.) November 17, 1897, p. 4. Item reprinted from the Casper *Wyoming Derrick*. Dan Sullivan, as we shall see, later became owner or part owner of the Bar C. Jack Allen was appointed Wyoming's top cop in the 1920s—state law enforcement commissioner—and later served as U.S. marshal and Natrona County sheriff.

26 Patterson, *Butch Cassidy*, after p. 155.

[27] Lamb, *Kid Curry*, 171-185 and notes, 341-343; Mokler, *History of Natrona County*, 318-323; Hanson, ed., *Powder River Country*, 453-456; bloodhound details from *Wyoming Derrick*, June 15, 1899, p. 1.

## Chapter 5: Through the 20th Century

[1] *Natrona County Tribune*, September 14, 1899. Cited in Rawson, *Looking for the End of the Rainbow*, p. 140 n. 81.

[2] Mrs. Richardson's cabin was the place Houck had bought from the Smiths, and where a bleeding Bob Smith was brought to die after the Hole-in-the-Wall Fight. It's perhaps a third of a mile downstream from the mouth of Buffalo Creek Canyon, and two miles southwest from the steep notch in the Red Wall now known as the Hole in the Wall. For decades, through a series of owners, the place was called the Hole in the Wall Ranch, or the Hole in the Wall cabin—not to be confused with the present Hole in the Wall Ranch, the former Bar C.

[3] Rawson, Elizabeth Lea. *Looking for the End of the Rainbow: Memoirs of Elizabeth Lea Rawson*, pp. 114-162, 181-185; Johnson County land records.

[4] Johnson County land records; Powder River Heritage Committee, *Our Powder River Heritage*, 209-210; Cheyenne *Sun-Leader*, Dec. 18 and Dec. 22, 1897. No trace at all of W.C. Alston, the other Bar C founder, could be found Johnson County land records.

[5] King and six other men were charged with rounding up hundreds of people willing to take $50 to perjure themselves by taking up 160-acre timber claims, and then signing the claims over to a syndicate. The syndicate then bundled the claims and sold them to a group of Scottish investors for $20 per acre. That is, each claim the syndicate illegally bought for $50 it sold to the Scots for $3,200. There were 600 claims in the deal. The case was reported widely in papers around

Wyoming and the West, and in the *New York Times*. A federal judge soon quashed the indictments, however, and the furor blew away. "Cute Californians Are Indicted for Stealing Government Land," *Cheyenne Democratic Leader*, April 4, 1886, p. 1; "The Redwood Timber Steal," Laramie *Weekly Boomerang*, April 8, 1886, p. 7; "Exposure and Nothing Beyond," New York *Times*, Nov. 22, 1886, p. 4.

6 "Sheep Raising," *Cheyenne Daily Sun*, April 20, 1895, p.3, citing the Paintrock Record. The NH was leased by well-known Natrona County pioneer Missou Hines.

7 *Natrona County Tribune,* July 15, 1897, p. 4; *Wyoming Derrick*, Dec. 9, 1897, p. 9; *Cheyenne Sun-Leader* Dec. 18, 1897, p. 9; *Cheyenne Sun-Leader* Dec. 22, 1897, p. 1; *Crook County Monitor*, Dec. 29, 1897, p. 1.

8 *Natrona County Tribune*, March 3, 1898, page 5.

9 Woods, *Sometimes the Books Froze, 35-36.* DeForest Richards served as Wyoming governor from 1899 to his death in April 1903.

10 "Trip to the Bighorn Mountains," *Wyoming Derrick*, Sept. 15, 1898, p. 8.

11 Power River Heritage Committee, *Our Powder River Heritage*, p. 209; *Wyoming Derrick*, June 6, 1899, p. 5; *Natrona County Tribune*, July 6, 1899, p. 5; *Natrona County Tribune*, June, 22, 1899, p. 5; *Wyoming Derrick*, October 5, 1899. p.4.

12 *Wyoming Derrick*, June 26, 1902, page 5; A Denver paper reported in December 1902 that the Bar C had been sold to Alex Ghent, the rustler who defied the Wilcox posse three years earlier; but he may only have bought land on Buffalo Creek a few miles south of the Bar C headquarters, where the log walls of a Ghent cabin remain; Ghent's name does not turn up on Johnson County land records of the

core holdings of the old Bar C in Section 13, T42N, R84W. Denver report cited in *Laramie Republican* Dec. 9, 1902. In 1906 King opened Shoshoni's first bank, in a fine gypsum-block building that later became the Yellowstone Drugstore, famous statewide for its malts and shakes, and is now on the National Historic Register.

13 *Buffalo Voice*, July 14, 1906, p. 2. The two Daniel Sullivans listed at the excellent genealogical website www.casperirish.com were both born in County Cork the early 1880s; one arrived in the states in 1906 and the other in 1907, making it highly unlikely either was this Dan Sullivan. Former Wyoming Governor Mike Sullivan, of Casper, claims no relation to this man. Most likely this Dan Sullivan was a relative of Patrick Sullivan, the former Casper mayor and future U.S. senator.

14 *Natrona County Tribune* Jan. 18, 1906, p. 5. The Kings' son, Leslie Lynch King, it seems appropriate to mention here, married Dorothy Gardner in Omaha Sept. 7, 1912. ("Leslie King to be Married," *Natrona County Tribune*, Aug. 28, 1912, p. 1.) Leslie Lynch King, Jr.—the future President Gerald Ford—was born in Omaha in July 1913. Leslie, Sr. proved jealous and extremely abusive, however. Dorothy King left her husband 16 days after the baby was born, returning eventually to live with her parents in Grand Rapids, Michigan, and obtained a divorce in December 1913. In 1916 she married Gerald Ford, and the future president took his stepfather's name. See Betty Ford, *The Times of My Life*, p. 1, Greene, *The Presidency of Gerald R. Ford,* pp. 44-45, and Funk, Josh. "Nebraska-Born, Ford Left State as Infant," Associated Press, Dec. 27, 2006. Fox News. Retrieved 1/27/10. Violence may have run in the family. Charles H. and Leslie King, Sr. were both accused in Omaha in November 1908 of badly beating John N. Bauer, an "expert wool sorter" at their wool warehouse, and permanently damaging his eye. Bauer sued them for $50,000. "Claims King Beat Him," *Riverton Republican*, Nov. 28, 1908, p. 1. C. H. King later called the lawsuit a

farce, saying "he had to fight Bauer or turn the business over to him and let him run it as he wanted to, so he knocked him down a couple of times and gave him a few kicks where it would do the most good…" "Says He Had to Fight," *Natrona County Tribune*, Dec. 16, 1908, p. 1.

15 "Townsite Company Files Incorporation." *Cheyenne Daily Leader*, Aug. 11, 1905, p. 8; "Consolidation Completed," *Riverton Republican* Aug. 1, 1908, p. 1.

16 Johnson County land records; *Our Powder River Heritage*, 209-210.

17 "Shearing at Casper," *Wyoming Derrick*, April 30, 1903, p. 1; "Central Wyoming Wool Sales," *Natrona County Tribune*, June 12, 1907, p. 1; *Natrona County Tribune*, Feb. 3, 1909, p. 5; "Has Been Prosperous Year," *Wyoming Tribune*, Nov. 11, 1907, p. 1. The house is now owned by the Shickich family.

18 John Wold notes from Joe Burke, 1994; *Our Powder River Heritage*, 209-210. "For the Flockmaster," *Northern Wyoming Herald*, Dec. 22, 1911, p. 8; *Kaycee Independent*, August 17, 1916, p. 3. Reps were advised to be at the Bar C by September 1, and to plan to be out six weeks, working the ranges south of the Middle Fork on Murphy and Willow Creeks, and on east to Salt Creek; *Casper Daily Tribune*, June 28, 1917, p. 5.

19 On the Cunninghams' Bar C social life, see *Cheyenne State Leader*, Sept. 22, 1920, p. 3; *Park County Enterprise*, Oct. 13, 1920, p. 1; *Northern Wyoming Stockman-Farmer*, Dec. 12, 1920, p. 4; *Casper Daily Tribune*, Sept. 20, 1921; *Wyoming Stockman-Farmer*, Oct. 1, 1921, p. 13; *Casper Daily Tribune*, October 6, 1921, p. 3, June 15, 1922, p. 3 and Sept. 9, 1922, p. 3; *Sheridan Post*, Oct. 3, 1922, p. 3; *Laramie Boomerang*, Sept. 26, 1922, p. 7; *Casper Herald*, Oct. 26,

1922, p.5; *Casper Daily Tribune*, November 1, 1922, p. 4; *Buffalo News* Nov. 19, 1925, p. 8; *Kaycee Optimist*, Feb. 5, 1926, p. 8; *Buffalo News*, Oct. 21, 1926, p. 5. Press reports noted the Careys met Esmonde on a trip to Ireland; it seems likely the Careys' connection to Esmonde was made through Horace Plunkett, still active in Irish politics at the time. Esmonde and Plunkett would have known each other as they were among a very few Irishmen to serve both in the British Parliament and in the Senate of the Irish Free State. Both their houses—Esmonde's family estate in County Wexford, and Plunkett's in County Meath—were among 300 burned in 1923 by anti-Treaty forces of the IRA.

[20] *Wyoming Sate Tribune*, Dec. 11, 1921; *New Castle News-Journal*, Feb. 23, 1922. Cunningham was on the board of the Wyoming Stockmen's Loan Company, which took loan applications from local banks, scrutinized them, and passed them along to the U.S. War Finance Corporation. Cunningham appeared before the corporation board in Washington to persuade its members that lending money on range land and dryland farms was a sound idea. The *New Castle News-Journal* hoped money would "flow more freely into the Rocky Mountain region after his visit."

[21] Interview with Casper sheep rancher Frank "Pinky" Ellis, Oct. 27, 2009; Garbutt and Morrison, *Casper Centennial*, 141.

[22] Johnson County land records; Garbutt and Morrison, *Casper Centennial*, 116-117, 141-143; *Powder River Heritage*, 213, 244; Ellis interviews, Oct. 27 and Nov. 10, 2009.

[23] Johnson County land records; Ellis interviews; Vaughn Cronin interview Nov. 16, 2009.

[24] "Hole-in-Wall Country Was Hiding Place for Outlaws," undated newspaper clipping apparently from a Casper newspaper, ca. 1949,

Hole-in-the-Wall file, Johnson County Library. "Oklahomans Buy Indian Ice Co." Casper Tribune-Herald, Aug. 28, 1951; "Hazel Katie Baxter," Casper Journal, Feb. 8-14, 2001.

[25] Johnson County land records; Connie Henry interview Dec. 15, 2009; Judy Middleton interview Dec. 16, 2009. "Historic Henning due for wrecker," *Casper Star-Tribune*, December 1972, clipping in Frances Seely Webb Collection, Casper College Western History Center; Pagna, Sammy. "Sons of the Pioneers Like it Fine Here," *Casper Morning Star*, August 15, 1953. "Frederick Michael 'Fred' Hartnett Jr., Casper Journal, June 15, 2000.

[26] Johnson County land records; Bonnie Culver interview, Dec. 9, 2009.

[27] Johnson County land records; Tat Yeigh interview, Dec. 29, 2009.

[28] Anne Mackinnon, "Water officials frustrated over Middle Fork archaeological rules," 11/24/85; "Morton opposed to Middle Fork dam; others imply interest," 12/6/85; "Water Commission postpones planning for Powder River Middle Fork dam, 3/22/86; Barron, "Legislative Panel votes to recommend construction of Middle Fork reservoir," 1/25/86. *Casper Star-Tribune*, Casper, Wyoming. The dam remains unbuilt due to insufficient demand for the water.

[29] Jack Wold interview, April 26, 2010

[30] Interviews with Bonnie Culver, 12/9/09; Bob Gosman, 12/2/09; John Wold, April 2009; Peter Wold, 4/16/09.

[31] Jim Richendifer interview, May 5, 2010;
http://www.vdar.com/PDF/09_WinterVanDyke.pdf, same date.

# Bibliography

Albanese, John, and Allen Darlington, William Eckerle, and Julie Francis. "48JO966: A New Bison Jump Site From the East Flank of the Bighorn Mountains, Johnson County, Wyoming" (paper presented at the 42nd Plains Archeology Conference, Iowa City, Iowa. October 1985.)

*Annual Report of the Commissioner of Indian Affairs, 1853*, 112-115, 354.

*Annual Report of the Commissioner of Indian Affairs, 1862,* 195.

Barron, Joan, "Legislative Panel votes to recommend construction of Middle Fork reservoir," 1/25/86. *Casper Star-Tribune*, Casper, Wyoming.

Bies, Mike. Interview March 2009.
Barry, Rev. J. Neilson. "The Trail of the Astorians." *The Quarterly of*

*the Oregon Historical Society*, xiii:3, (September 1912), 227-239.

Bearss, Edwin C. *Bighorn Canyon National Recreation Area, Montana-Wyoming: history basic data.* U.S. Office of History and Historic Architecture, Eastern Service Center, 1970. 2 vols.

Berry, Don. *A Majority of Scoundrels: An Informal History of the Rocky Mountain Fur Company.* New York: Harper & Brothers, 1961.

Blenkinsop, Willis. "Edward Rose." Hafen, LeRoy R., ed. *The Mountain Men and the Fur Trade of the Far West.* Glendale, Cal.: The Arthur H. Clark Company, 1972. Volume ix, 335-345.

Brayer, Herbert O. "The 76 Ranch on Powder River: Herbert O. Brayer Sketches Career of Moreton Frewen, English Cattle King, and his Experiences in Early-Day Wyoming." *The Westerners Brand Book*, Chicago corral, vii:10 (1950) 73-75, 77-80.

Burgan, Scott. Sheridan, Wyoming. Personal conversation 2/11/09 and emails, 2/11/09 and 3/4/09.

Burroughs, John Rolfe. *Guardian of the Grasslands: The First Hundred Years of the Wyoming Stock Growers Association.* Cheyenne: Pioneer Printing and Stationery Co., 1971.

Burns, Robert Homer, Andrew Springs Gillespie, Willing Gay Richardson. *Wyoming's Pioneer Ranches.* Laramie: Top-of-the-World Press, 1955.

Chittenden, Hiram Martin. *The American Fur Trade of the Far West.* Stanford, California: Academic Reprints, 1954. First published 1902. 2 vols.

Condit, Thelma Gatchell. "The Hole-in-the-Wall: Part 1, Location and

Origin of Name." *Annals of Wyoming* 27:2 (October 1955),136-141.

_____. "The Hole-in-the-Wall: Part II—The Indians," *Annals of Wyoming*, 28:1 (April 1956), 27-40.

_____. "The Hole-in-the-Wall: Part IV—The Big Cow Outfits," *Annals of Wyoming*, 29:1 (April 1957), 41-65.

_____. "The Hole-in-the-Wall: Part V, Section 1: Outlaws and Rustlers," *Annals of Wyoming* 29:2 (October 1957), 160-176.

_____. "The Hole-in-the-Wall: Part V, Section 2: Outlaws and Rustlers," *Annals of Wyoming* 30:1 (April 1958), 17-36.

_____. "The Hole-in-the-Wall: Part V, Section 2: Outlaws and Rustlers," *Annals of Wyoming* 30:2 (October 1958), 175-192.

_____. "The Hole-in-the-Wall: Part V, Section 4: Outlaws and Rustlers," *Annals of Wyoming* 31:1 (April 1959), 53-75.

_____. "The Hole-in-the-Wall: Part VII, Section 3: Early Day Dances," *Annals of Wyoming* 33:2 (October 1961), 178-192.

_____. "The Wolfers." *Frontier Times* 32:4 (Fall 1958), 16-18; 33-36.

Cronin, Bernard (Barney). Taped interview, 1997, with Donna Gowin Johnston for her book, *The 33-Mile Road (of Natrona County, Wyoming): My Story*. Published by author, 2006.
Cronin, Vaughn. Interview, November 6, 2009.

Culver, Bonnie. Interview, December 9, 2009.

David, Robert B. *Malcolm Campbell, Sheriff.* Casper, Wyo.: Wyomingiana, Inc., 1932.

Denig, Edwin Thompson. *Five Indian Tribes of the Upper Missouri: Sioux, Arickaras, Assiniboines, Crees, Crows.* Edited, with an introduction by John C. Ewers. Norman: University of Oklahoma Press, 1961.

DeVoe, Mrs. Henry [May]. "Some Reminiscences." Two-page account in Johnson County (Wyoming) Library. No date.

DeVoto, Bernard, *Across the Wide Missouri.* New York: Bonanza Books, 1972. First published 1947 by Houghton Mifflin.

_____, ed., *Journals of Lewis and Clark,* Boston: Houghton Mifflin, 1953.

Digby, Margaret. *Horace Plunkett, an Anglo-American Irishman.* Oxford: Blackwell, 1949.

Dobyns, Henry F. "Native American Trade Centers as Contagious Disease Foci." *Disease and Demography in the Americas,* edited by John W. Verano and Douglas H. Ubelaker. Washington: Smithsonian Institution Press, 1992, 215-222.

Dodge, Richard Irving. *The Powder River Expedition Journals of Colonel Richard Irving Dodge,* edited by Wayne K. Kime. Norman: University of Oklahoma Press, 1997.

Doyle, Susan Badger. *Journeys to the Land of Gold: Emigrant Diaries from the Bozeman Trail.* Helena: Montana Historical Society Press,

2000. 2 volumes.

Dunlay, Thomas W. *Wolves for the Blue Soldiers: Indian Scouts and Auxiliaries with the United States Army, 1860-1890.* Lincloln: University of Nebraska Press, 1982.

Earle, B.J. Interview, March 2009.

Ellis, Frank "Pinky." Interviews, October 27 and November 10, 2009

Ford, Betty, with Chris Chase. *The Times of My Life.* New York: Harper & Row, 1978.

Francis, Julie. "Imagery of Medicine Lodge," chapter 9 in George Frison and Danny Walker, eds., *Medicine Lodge Creek: Holocene Archeology of the Big Horn Basin, Wyoming*, vol. 1, 209-226. Clovis Press, 2007.

_____. "Powder River—Let 'Er Buck: Ten Thousand Years of Hunter-Gatherer Prehistory on the Middle Fork Reservoir, Wyoming" (paper presented at the 51st annual meeting of the Society for American Archeology, New Orleans, April 1986).

_____. "The Middle Fork of the Powder River: 1947-1985." *North Dakota Archaeology*, vol. 5, 1994, 177-189.

_____. Interviews, December 18, 2008 and January 26, 2009.

Frink, Maurice. *Cow Country Cavalcade: Eighty Years of the Wyoming Stock Growers Association.* Denver: Old West Pub., 1954.

Frison, Paul. *Calendar of Change.* Worland, Wyoming: Serlkay, Inc., 1975. Copyright by author.

Garbutt, Irving and Chuck Morrison. *Casper Centennial, 1889-1989;*

*Natrona County, Wyoming, 1890-1990: featuring also geological record, prehistoric man, first settlers*. Dallas, Texas: Curtis Media Corporation, 1990.

Gosman, Robert. Interview, December 2, 2009.

Greene, Jerome A. *Lakota and Cheyenne: Indian Views of the Great Sioux War*. Norman: University of Oklahoma Press, 2000.

Greene, Jerome A. *Morning Star Dawn: the Powder River Expedition and the Northern Cheyennes, 1876*. Norman: University of Oklahoma Press, 2003.

Greene, John Robert. *The Presidency of Gerald Ford*. Lawrence: University Press of Kansas, 1995.

Grinnell, George Bird. *The Fighting Cheyennes*. Norman: University of Oklahoma Press, 1956. First pub. 1915, by Charles Scribner's Sons.

Hanson, Margaret Brock, ed. *Powder River Country: The Papers of J. Elmer Brock*. Cheyenne: Frontier Printing, 1981. Second edition, 1989.

Henry, Connie Hartnett. Interview, Dec. 15, 2009.

Holmes, Reuben. "The Five Scalps," ed. Stella M. Drumm, Missouri Historical Society, *Glimpses of the Past 5*, (January-March, 1938); 3-54.

Hyde, George E. *Life of George Bent, Written from his Letters*. Edited by Savoie Lottinville. Norman: University of Oklahoma Press, 1968. Irving, Washington. *Astoria, or Anecdotes of an Enterprise Beyond the Rocky Mountains*. Edited with an introduction by Edgeley W. Todd. Norman: University of Oklahoma Press, 1964.

Jewett, Wayne. "Marie Dorion and the Astoria Expedition." *Wild West*, October 2000, accessed 2/20/10 at http://www.historynet.com/marie-dorion-and-the-astoria-expedition.htm

Kelly, Charles. The Outlaw Trail: A History of Butch Cassidy and his Wild Bunch. New York: Bonanza Books, 1959.

Lamb, F. Bruce. *Kid Curry: The Life and Times of Harvey Logan and the Wild Bunch: An Old West Narrative*. Boulder, Colorado: Johnson Books, 1991.

_____. *The Wild Bunch: A Selected Critical Annotated Bibliography of the Literature.* Worland, Wyoming: High Plains Publishing Company, Inc., 1993.

Leibrand, Gary. "Wyoming's Hole in the Wall Ranch: putting VDAR genetics to the test in tough country," VanDyke Angus Ranch, Winter 2009, accessed 11/29/10 at:
http://www.vdar.com/PDF/09_WinterVanDyke.pdf.

Leonard, Zenas. *Narrative of the Adventures of Zenas Leonard, fur trader and trapper, 1831-1835*. Accessed 2/20/10 at:
http://www.xmission.com/~drudy/mtman/html/leonintr.html

Loendorf, Larry, and Julie Francis. "Three Rock Art Sites on the Middle Fork of the Powder River, Wyoming." *Archaeology in Montana*, 28:2, 1987, 18-24.

Lott, Howard B., ed. "Diary of Major Wise, Hunting Trip in Powder River Country in 1880." *Annals of Wyoming*, 12:2, April 1940. 85-118.

MacKinnon, Anne. "Water officials frustrated over Middle Fork archaeological rules," 11/24/85; "Morton opposed to Middle Fork dam; others imply interest," 12/6/85; "Water Commission postpones planning for Powder River Middle Fork dam, 3/22/86; *Casper Star-Tribune*, Casper, Wyoming.

Mann, Charles C. *1491: New Revelations of the Americas before Columbus*. New York: Vintage Books, 2006.

McCleary, Timothy P. *The Stars We Know: Crow Indian Astronomy and Lifeways*. Prospect Heights, Illinois: Waveland Press, Inc. 1997.

McDermott, Fred. "A Misunderstood Term." Interview of Fred McDermott of Glendo, Wyoming, ca. 1938, by Minnie Rietz. Wyoming State Archives, WPA file #899.

Mercer, A.S. *The Banditti of the Plains, or the Cattlemen's Invasion of Wyoming in 1892: the Crowning Infamy of the Ages*. Norman: University of Oklahoma Press, 1954.

Middleton, Judy Hartnett. Interview, Dec. 16, 2009.

Millais, Geoffrey. Correspondence 1885-1886, American Heritage Center, University of Wyoming.

Missouri Basin Project, "Appraisal of the Archaeological and Paleontological Resources of the Middle Fork Area, Johnson County, Wyoming." Smithsonian Institution, Washington, D.C., 1953.

Mokler, Alfred James. *History of Natrona County, Wyoming, 1888-1922: true portrayal of the yesterdays of a new county and a typical frontier town of the Middle West*. Ann Arbor, Mich.: for University Microfilms by Argonaut Press, 1966. First published 1923 by R.R. Donnelly and Sons, Chicago.

Myers, Sue and Patty Myers. *Tales of the Trails: a history and stories of the Big Horn Mountain Stockdrives*. Wyoming Centennial Commission: 1990.

Nicholas, Liza J. *Becoming Western: Stories of Culture and Identity in the Cowboy State*. Lincoln: University of Nebraska Press, 2006, 1-32.

Old Horn, Dale D. and Tim McCleary. "Ethnographic Setting" in *The Apsáalooke*, accessed 11/29/10 at: http://lib.lbhc.cc.mt.us/about/genealogy/kinship2.php.

Patterson, Richard. *Butch Cassidy: A Biography*. Lincoln: Bison Books, University of Nebraska Press, 1998.

Peterson, Gary. "Antonio Montero and the Portuguese Houses: An Outpost on Powder River." *Rocky Mountain Fur Trade Journal* vol. 2, 2008, 31-47. Published by the Museum of the Mountain Man, Pinedale, Wyoming.

Powder River Heritage Committee. *Our Powder River Heritage*. Kaycee, Wyoming: Powder River Heritage Committee, 1982.

Powell, Peter John. *People of the Sacred Mountain: a History of the Northern Cheyenne Chiefs and Warrior Societies with an Epilogue, 1969-1974*. 2 vols. San Francisco: Harper and Row, 1981.

Rawson, Elizabeth Lea. *Looking for the End of the Rainbow: Memoirs of Elizabeth Lea Rawson*. Edited by Merle Ann Kimball. Baltimore: Gateway Press, 2005.

Robertson, R.G. *Rotting Face: Smallpox and the American Indian*. Caldwell, Idaho: Caxton Press, 2001.
Sandoz, Mary. *Cheyenne Autumn*. New York: Hastings House, 1975. First published 1953.
Savage, William Woodrow, Jr. *Cattle King: Sir Horace Plunkett in*

*Wyoming, 1879-1889*. M.A. Thesis, University of South Carolina, 1966.

Sheridan, Philip H. and W.T. Sherman. *Reports of Inspection made in the summer of 1877 by Generals P.H. Sheridan and W.T. Sherman of country north of the Union Pacific Railroad.* United States War Department, Government Printing Office, 1878.

Shields, George O. (Coquina). *Hunting in the Great West (Rustlings in the Rockies): hunting and fishing by mountain and stream.* (Fireside series) New York (?): Donohue Brothers, 1883.

Smith, Helena Huntington. "The Truth about the Hole-in-the-Wall Fight." Montana the Magazine of Western History, xi:3, 11-19.

_____. *The War on Powder River: The History of an Insurrection.* Lincoln: University of Nebraska Press, 1966. Bison Book edition, 1967.

Smith, Sherry L. *Sagebrush Soldier: Private William Earl Smith's View of the Sioux War of 1876.* Norman: University of Oklahoma Press, 1989.

Stands in Timber, John and Margot Liberty, with the assistance of Robert Utley. *Cheyenne Memories.* Lincoln: University of Nebraska Press, 1972, c1967 by Yale University.

Stuart, Robert. *The Discovery of the Oregon Trail: Robert Stuart's Narratives of his Overland Trip Eastward from Astoria in 1812-13.* Edited by Philip Ashton Rollins. New York: Scribner's Sons, 1935. Introduction to Bison Books edition by Howard Lamar copyright by University of Nebraska Press. First Bison Book printing 1995.

Sweem, Glenn. Oral histories, 2/4/96, 4/22/96, and 5/3/96, tapes and transcripts at Western History Collection, Sheridan County Fulmer Public Library, Sheridan, Wyoming.

_____. (probably. Article is unsigned.) "The Sweem-Taylor Site, 48 JO 301," *Wyoming Archaeologist*, II:10, November, 1959, pp. 4-8.

Taylor, Colin. Interview, 9/16/09.

Trimble, Michael K. "The 1832 Inoculation Program on the Missouri River." *Disease and Demography in the Americas,* edited by John W. Verano and Douglas H. Ubelaker. Washington: Smithsonian Institution Press, 1992. 257-264.

Utley, Robert. *A Life Wild and Perilous: Mountain Men and the Paths to the Pacific*. New York: Henry Holt & Co., 1997.

Victor, Frances Fuller. *The River of the West: The Adventures of Joe Meek*, vol. 1. Missoula: Mountain Press Publishing Company, 1983. First published 1870.

Werner, Fred H *The Dull Knife Battle: Doomsday for the Northern Cheyennes*. Greeley, Colorado: Werner Publications, 1981.

Wentworth, Edward Norris. *America's Sheep Trails*: *History, Personalities*. Ames, Iowa. The Iowa State College Press, 1948.

West, Trevor. *Horace Plunkett: Cooperation and Politics: an Irish biography*, Gerrards Cross, Buckinghamshire: C. Smythe, 1986.

Wister, Owen. *Owen Wister Out West: His Journals and Letters*, edited by Fannie Kimble Wister. Chicago: University of Chicago Press, 1958.
Wold, Jack. Interview, April 26, 2010.
Wold, John. Interview, April 2009.

Wold, Peter. Interview April 16, 2009.

Wood, W. Raymond and Thomas D. Thiessen, editors. *Early Fur Trade on the Northern Plains: Canadian Traders Among the Mandan and Hidatsa Indians, 1738-1818: The Narratives of John Macdonnell, Francois-Antoine Larocque, David Thompson, Charles McKenzie.* Norman: University of Oklahoma, 1985.

Woods, Lawrence M. *British Gentlemen in the Wild West: The Era of the Intensely English Cowboy.* New York: The Free Press, a division of MacMillan, Inc., 1989.

Woods, L. Milton. *Moreton Frewen's Western Adventures.* Boulder, Colo.: Roberts Rinehart, Inc. for the American Heritage Center, University of Wyoming, 1986.

_____. *Sometimes the Books Froze: Wyoming's Economy and its Banks.* Boulder: Colorado Associated University Press, 1985.

Wyoming Pioneer Association, Heritage Book Committee. *Pages from Converse County's Past.* Douglas: Wyoming Historical Press, 1986.

Wyoming Stock Growers Association. Correspondence and executive committee minutes, 1886. In WSGA collection, American Heritage Center, University of Wyoming.

Yeigh, Arlene "Tat." Interview, December 29, 2009.

# A HISTORY

# About the Author

Tom Rea is a writer and editor in Casper, Wyoming. His previous books include *Bone Wars: The Excavation and Celebrity of Andrew Carnegie's Dinosaur* (University of Pittsburgh Press, 2001, 2004) and *Devil's Gate: Owning the Land, Owning the Story* (University of Oklahoma Press, 2006.)

Index

.

www.ingramcontent.com/pod-product-compliance
Lightning Source LLC
Chambersburg PA
CBHW052035090426
42739CB00010B/1921